WHO WAS EDGAR CAYCE?

Edgar Cayce was born in 1877 in Hopkinsville, Kentucky and lived sixty-seven years that were sometimes painfully eventful, but tremendously enlightening. He had developed a gift in former lifetimes which gave him the capacity in this life to enter a state of altered consciousness. He was able to be in touch with the akashic records and the information in what he called the Universal Consciousness.

In his state of altered consciousness, Cayce would respond to questions and often would give special dissertations on a variety of subjects. Two thirds of his nearly 15,000 readings had to do with healing of the human body. He is well-known, too, for his predictions on earth changes and with readings on reincarnation, dreams, soul development, Christ consciousness, astrology, Atlantis, ancient Egypt, and emotional development. Cayce's readings evidenced a very close relationship with Jesus and his teachings, and it is not surprising that he advised hundreds who sought his counsel to take Jesus as their pattern for living in these troublesome times.

Cayce could also contact the unconscious mind of individuals far distant from where he was giving a reading, and could describe not only their past lives, but also the state of the inquirer's physiological functioning and what needed to be done to return that individual to full health.

Cayce's legacy for the world can be found not only in the hearts and minds of millions of individuals whose lives he has changed, but also at the Association for Research and Enlightenment (A.R.E.) Library in Virginia Beach, VA which houses the Cayce Readings.

Edgar Cayce called his work the work of the Christ, and anyone who studies these readings to any depth will most likely agree.

William A. McGarey, M.D.

MYSTERIES OF
ATLANTIS
REVISITED

EDGAR EVANS CAYCE
GAIL CAYCE SCHWARTZER
DOUGLAS G. RICHARDS

St. Martin's Paperbacks

Unless otherwise noted, Scripture quotations contained herein are from the Revised Standard Version of the Bible, copyrighted 1946, 1952, 1971 by the Division of Christian Education of the National Council of the Churches of Christ in the U.S.A., and are used by permission. All rights reserved.

Figure 5-2 is from Dolphin, L. T., and N. Bakarat, *Electromagnetic Sounder Experiments at the Pyramids of Giza*. Menlo Park, CA: SRI International, 1975. Reprinted by permission of SRI International.

Figures 5-4 and 5-5 were provided courtesy of H. Haas, J. Devine, P. Wenke, M. Lehner, W. Wolfli, and G. Bonani.

Figures and quotations in Chapter 7 are from *Vulnerability of Energy Distribution Systems to an Earthquake in the Eastern United States—An Overview*. Washington, DC: American Association of Engineering Societies, 1986. Reprinted by permission of J. E. Beavers.

MYSTERIES OF ATLANTIS REVISITED

Library of Congress Catalog Card Number: 88-45129

ISBN: 0-312-96153-7

Printed in the United States of America

Harper & Row trade paperback edition published in 1988
St. Martin's Paperbacks edition/March 1997

10 9 8 7 6 5 4 3 2 1

*To Hugh Lynn Cayce,
for his inspiration and guidance of all those
who sought to learn from the Cayce readings*

CONTENTS

FOREWORD

A PERSONAL REMEMBRANCE OF EDGAR CAYCE

MY LAST MEMORIES of my father, Edgar Cayce, are of a slender man, slightly over six feet tall. His piercing, gray eyes still sparkled through the rimless glasses he wore. His hair was gray and thinning and he had developed a paunch from too much of Mother's good cooking and not enough time for exercise. An eager fisherman, an avid gardener, a proficient carpenter—my father was all of these. But he had less and less time for many of these things he liked to do as more and more people learned of his unique psychic abilities and sought him out for "readings."

The readings were strange and wonderful to those who got them, but I grew up with and accepted them as common, everyday occurrences. I had both physical and life readings from Dad, and now and then I listened to the ones he gave for strangers. Nonetheless I looked forward more to the times we could spend together fishing or working on a carpentry project.

Neither I nor my brother Hugh Lynn ever shared Dad's enthusiasm for gardening. Our lack of interest never deterred him, though, and he was continually hoeing around some new tree or shrub he had planted, or weeding his garden. He would rather spend money on a load of topsoil than on food for the table—and frequently did, much to the consternation of Mother. We lived in several homes in Virginia Beach, Virginia, leaving a trail of fruit trees, rose bushes, and grapevines behind us. Everything seemed to grow well for Edgar Cayce. I suspected that some of his psychic powers seeped over into his workaday world, because I never knew him to return empty handed from a fishing trip or with empty arms from his garden.

Money, however, was another matter. He always seemed broke and could never accumulate any. It slipped through his fingers like sand from the beach.

Before we came to Virginia Beach, we had moved from Selma, Alabama, to Dayton, Ohio. I remember a particularly cold day in Dayton, when Dad stuffed newspapers in my shirt and pants to keep out the cold wind because I didn't have a coat. My thin clothes were not designed for northern winters. I nearly froze that winter in Dayton, and was overjoyed when we moved south to Virginia.

In spite of our somewhat less than affluent living conditions, the early years at Virginia Beach were filled with fun for the whole family. In the winter, we hauled pound poles (long pine poles that had broken away from staked-out fishing nets) off the beach and sawed them into firewood. We would sit around the fire while the northeast wind howled outside. Dad would tell stories or all the family would play Parcheesi. Through these family conversations, I learned how Dad had developed his psychic talents and why he would never use them to make money.

Edgar Cayce was born near Hopkinsville, Kentucky, in 1877. He had had some strange experiences as a child, and his first "reading" was for himself. While working as a clerk in a bookstore, the young Cayce had lost his voice. None of the local doctors had been able to help him. In desperation, he turned to a man who had been experimenting with the new fad of hypnotism. With the aid of the hypnotist, Cayce was able—of his own volition—to put himself into a sleep-like state. The hypnotist encouraged him to describe his condition and suggest a remedy, and Cayce began to speak from his autohypnotic state. He described a remedy for his condition that did indeed restore his voice.

A local doctor who observed Cayce's performance became interested. He thought it was only a step from diagnosing himself to diagnosing the ailments of others. These experiments proved successful, and the doctor's success and Cayce's fame spread as a result of Cayce's accurate diagnosing or "reading" of his patients. The word "reading" stuck, and Cayce's discourses from his sleep-like state became known as readings.

At first Cayce was wary of his own ability, afraid he would somehow be wrong, and that someone might suffer as a result of a wrong diagnosis. His worst fears never materialized; and instead of suffering, more and more people found relief by following the suggestions in his physical readings.

Cayce never remembered anything he said in his trance-like sleeps. His words were taken down in shorthand and later typed. Therefore Cayce never knew the questions he was asked at the conclusion of a reading before he was given the suggestion to awaken. Occasionally, the person conducting the reading sought personal gain, and would inquire about the future outcome of a horse race or seek investment advice concerning the stock or commodity markets. Cayce would answer the questions to the inquirer's profit, but he would awaken nervous and tired, usually with painful headaches.

When Cayce learned how he was being used, he gave up "psychic readings" and devoted himself entirely to working as a photographer, a job in which he literally had his trials by fire. A fire burned him out of business, leaving him deeply in debt. On another occasion, an exploding can of photographer's flash powder burned Hugh Lynn's eyes. The doctors suggested the removal of one eye and declared he would probably not be able to see out of the remaining one. Dad was distraught. As a last resort, he turned again to trying a "reading" for Hugh Lynn. The reading outlined a treatment that not only saved both of Hugh Lynn's eyes, but restored his vision.

Encouraged by this remarkable success, Cayce began again to give readings. However, in order to avoid the problems he had encountered before, he insisted that his wife always conduct the reading. From that time on my mother, Gertrude, was the one who gave him the suggestion for the reading; she was the one who asked the questions and she was the one who gave him the suggestion to wake up.

For the next twenty-seven years, thousands of people found relief from pain and suffering by following the suggestions of Edgar Cayce's readings. The records on file in the Association for Research and Enlightenment (A.R.E.) library in Virginia Beach testify to his accuracy. Doctors' reports and patients' case histories are there for all to see. As the many books and articles about him conclude, Edgar Cayce was undoubtedly an amazingly precise psychic diagnostician. As an example of a physical reading, let me tell you of a personal experience.

In 1934, at the age of sixteen, I was practicing football. I attempted to block a fellow teammate nearly twice my size. It was a poor block, because I left my feet in an effort to knock him down. He raised his knee to ward off my flying body, and his knee pad caught the front part of my hip bone. Pain shot through my whole body and my leg went numb from the hip down. I was out of football for the rest of the season, limping around with a sore hip, until I got help from my father through a reading. The reading said,

> With special reference to the right side or hip, we find there has been an injury to the covering of the pelvis bone ... with a straining in the muscular forces of the membranes and muscles that cover, or that are contingent to, those portions of same. It is rather inflammation to the *covering* or skin covering of the bone itself.
>
> As we find, to prevent trouble of inflammation arising to such an extent as to cause disorders or troubles later on ... or to prevent such inflammation as to disturb the activity of the muco-membranes of the diaphragm itself, or the covering, or the diaphragm of the lower intestinal body itself, there should be applied that which will absorb or reduce the tendency for the accumulation of thickened tissue ... or what may be properly called a condition where tissue, inflammation, and roughness cause adhesions. See?
>
> Then, we would massage the side thoroughly with a combination made in the form of a lotion.
>
> To one ounce of pure olive oil (heated, not to boiling but heated) add, while the olive oil is still warm, and stir into same in *this* manner this quantity, and in the order as given:
>
> Tincture of Benzoin .... ½ ounce,
> Tincture of Myrrh .... ¼ ounce,
> Russian White Oil .... ½ ounce,

Witchhazel.......................... ¼ ounce,
Oil of Sassafras................ 2 to 3 minims.

Use this night and morning to massage over the right
side covering the caecum area, and also over all portions
of the pelvis bone, see? Over the upper part to the lower
portion of the sacral area; the caecum, the pelvis bone,
to the lower portion of the sacral area, on the right side.

Be mindful that the eliminations are kept well in hand;
sufficient activity of the intestinal system to allay those
things that may be thrown off into the circulation.

Do not *strain* the body, until these conditions are reduced.

[Mother asked if I should refrain from all exercise.]
No. Just don't *strain* that side, as in scuffling or wres-
tling or the like.

I followed the suggestions given in the reading for four or
five months. The pain in my hip lessened, but a slight soreness
remained. Dad gave me another reading, which advised me to
be persistent. He said the condition had improved, but that it
would take time to heal entirely. I persisted and obtained complete relief. I was able to play baseball, basketball, and tennis
with no ill effects. For me, Edgar Cayce's readings were very
effective. They gave me back the full use of my leg.

The physical readings make up about 60 percent of Edgar
Cayce's fourteen thousand or so readings. There are a number
of minor categories such as business advice and dream interpretation, but by far the next largest category, approximately
20 percent of the total, are life readings. These readings dealt
with psychological rather than physical problems. They attempted to answer questions people might have about voca-
tional problems, their purpose in life, and marriage and human
relations. The first life reading came about in this manner:

In the early 1920s, a man with an insatiable inquisitiveness
about metaphysics opened a new dimension for Cayce and his
psychic readings. In an attempt to obtain an astrological hor-
oscope from Cayce, Arthur Lammers was told that the effect
of the stars and planets on a person's life was not nearly as
influential as the effect of that person's past life upon his pres-

ent one. Cayce then proceeded to give Lammers an account of his previous lives.

When Cayce awoke and heard what he had said, he was dumbfounded. Awake, he knew as little about reincarnation and the occult as he knew about medicine. Was it possible that reincarnation could be true? How did it fit in with his Bible teachings and Christian roots? Cayce wasn't sure. Abstract questions of philosophic systems had never concerned him. He was well versed in Christianity and the Bible, but he had never studied other world religions. He was ignorant of the fact that reincarnation was a cardinal belief in the teachings of Hinduism and Buddhism.

Between 1923 and 1924, when Cayce was awash in waves of doubt about this new information from his unconscious, I was only five and six years old. I missed all the lively arguments between Lammers and Cayce, and the long philosophic family discussions. I did accompany the family to Dayton, Ohio, where Lammers sponsored our family's room and board to satisfy his thirst for knowledge. What convinced Dad that these new "life readings" were factual? Was it the philosophic discussions with the knowledgeable Lammers? Was it the concurrence of information, given for complete strangers, with verifiable facts? Or was it the manner in which the readings integrated Christian ideals into the framework of reincarnation? Each argument probably carried weight, but I suspect that the latter had the greatest influence.

Whatever the reason, Edgar Cayce became convinced that the life readings were as helpful as the physical diagnoses. They seemed to harm no one, so he continued to give them on request. He came to feel that the life readings were given to help an individual understand and answer questions and problems about his or her present life, and that to obtain a life reading for frivolous reasons was a waste of time. His readings expressed this view as follows:

> Do not gain knowledge only to thine own undoing. Remember Adam. Do not obtain that which ye cannot make constructive in thine own experience and in the experience of those whom ye contact day by day. Do not attempt to force, impel, or even try to impress thy

knowledge upon another—in the studies, then, know where ye are going. To gain knowledge merely for thine own satisfaction is a thing, a condition, an experience to be commended, if it does not produce in thine experience a feeling or a manner of expression that ye are better than another on account of thy knowledge. This becomes self-evident that it would become then a stumbling block, unless ye know what ye will do with thy knowledge.

. . . For to find only that ye lived, died, and were buried under the cherry tree in grandmother's garden does not make thee one whit a better neighbor, citizen, mother, or father. But to know that ye spoke unkindly and suffered for it, and in the present may correct it by being righteous—*that* is worthwhile. What is righteousness? Just being kind, just being noble, just being self-sacrificing, just being willing to be the hands for the blind, the feet for the lame—these are constructive experiences. Ye may gain knowledge of same, for incarnations are a fact. How may ye prove it? In thy daily living. (no. 5753–2, June 29, 1937)*

My father was not always deadly serious. Asleep or awake, he exhibited a sense of humor and a ready wit. He did not hesitate to chide a patient who asked foolish questions or pretended to have followed suggestions when he really had not. For example, in a business reading a patient was beginning a question: "The advice of the forces has been followed during the past week—" [Cayce interrupting] "Not very well!" (no. 257–137, August 7, 1934).

The same person, in a later reading, prefaced a question

---

*Each of the Edgar Cayce readings has been assigned a two-part number to provide easy reference. Each person who received a reading was given an anonymous number; this is the first half of the two-part number. Since many individuals obtained more than one reading, the second number designates the number of that reading in the series. Reading no. 5753–2 was given for a person who was assigned case number 5753. This particular reading was the second one that person obtained from Cayce.

with the statement: "Since I have complied with the instructions in the last reading—" [Cayce again interrupting] "Partially!" (no. 257–151, June 22, 1935).

This man was slow to follow Cayce's advice. Seventeen readings later, he stated, "Well, we have asked for guidance and will follow it." "Well, it has been given about forty times what you should do and you haven't done it yet!" (no. 257–168, July 2, 1936).

Many of Cayce's twits and banter were in the form of terse comments. In answer to a question about a rub: "Rub this on the outside?" Cayce replied, "You can't rub it on the inside!" (no. 34–7, June 9, 1911). And in answer to a question about how a medicine should be taken: "Just how should the Bromo Quinine be taken?" "Swallow it!" (no. 528–15, January 17, 1938).

There are countless other examples of Cayce's appreciation of a sense of humor. In many readings, he suggested the importance of humor as a factor in keeping one's health.

The sort of information contained in a life reading is clear in the following example. The patient's name has been replaced by his case number, 2962. The reading noted the characteristic of preoccupation or indifference:

> [2962 is] one that apparently many times, even in company with others, will appear to be preoccupied. . . . One often, from the manner or mien, that may appear to others—with whom it might be associated, either in a business or a social way—as one very indifferent as to this or that conclusion that might be reached, or as to the relationships that might grow out of any contact.
>
> . . . One that is interested in many things; likes to read a good book; likes the interpreting of puzzles, quizzes or the like—at times, and at others they are rather boresome to the entity.
>
> . . . One that is very interested in things of the unseen, or the occult, or psychic side of life; yet one who would appear to be rather close in observation and yet granting much that others would not even consider as to being granted.
>
> . . . For, the characteristics become rather of the spec-

ulative nature on the part of others. While the entity is a good spender, rarely is it said to be a good active force in controlling interests. And yet in those things of mechanical nature, or those that have to do with transportation, or of such natures, would be channels through which the entity might find the opportunity for the greater privileges, or the greater experiences in this particular sojourn.

[The reading gave four previous incarnations. The most recent was among the early settlers of New York, the second in England during the Crusades, the third among the Israelites journeying out of Egypt, and the fourth in prehistoric Egypt. From the incarnation in England came an interest in communications and things of a mechanical nature, which was said to be an influence in the present.]

... The entity then showed its leaning toward the preparation of things of the mechanical nature—as communications, as would be expressed in the present telegraphy or in radio, or in communications of any nature for the distribution either of definite products of a given vicinity or of those that might be to the common good of all.

... And in those fields of service that would have to do with communications—planes, wires, or radio, any or all of these—there will be offered particular advantages to the entity. (no. 2962–1, April 13, 1943)

At the time of the reading, the subject was in the Canadian army. In the request for the reading, he had stated that he was married, but separated from his wife. He did not submit any questions. After receiving the reading, 2962 wrote to Edgar Cayce and thanked him for the information. He admitted an interest in the occult, an interest in puzzles, and mechanical aptitude; but he said that in the case of radio and television, he was becoming more interested in how the material was prepared and presented than in the mechanics of it.

Nothing more was heard until thirty-three years later. Mr. 2962 had died, but before that he had remarried. His second wife was still living and had come in contact with the Association for Research and Enlightenment (A.R.E.) through an A.R.E. regional representative. She mentioned that her former husband, Mr. 2962, had had a life reading. My daughter, Gail Cayce Schwartzer, who worked for the Edgar Cayce Foundation at the time, wrote the woman in hopes that she might verify some of the statements mentioned in Mr. 2962's life reading. The following extracts from the woman's reply illustrate Cayce's accuracy. About his preoccupation and indifference, she commented,

[2962] was not particularly shy but often appeared to be so because of his seeming to be withdrawn. Before we were married, when we were both working at the same television station, I had been told by a salesman that [2962] sometimes appeared not to be paying attention when he was trying to discuss a business matter with him. I mentioned this as tactfully as I could, in hope that [2962] would perhaps change his behavior. Although we laughed about it, he insisted that he could think of more than one thing at a time, and that he was indeed paying attention, even when he seemed not to be. My own opinion is that he sometimes became absorbed in his thoughts and was guilty of what he was being accused of. But he was not indifferent. He was, if anything, one of the most considerate people I have ever known.

[The reading had also stated that fields of service having to do with communications—planes, wires, radio—would offer advantages to 2962. His wife confirmed that he had done some broadcasting in London during World War II, and later became a television director in the United States. She said he was intensely interested in all visual media and had moved from an interest in theater to film and television.] *It was not just a way to make a living but was his prime interest.*

[Furthermore, she said that [2962] liked books, quizzes, and puzzles and was very interested in the occult or psychic side of life.] Great ability in mechanical things. One comment by a cameraman with whom he worked has always meant a great deal to me. He said, "[2962]

asks us to do the impossible, and then shows us how to do it.''

The preceding life reading and comments are not meant as proof of reincarnation, but as an example of a life reading and evidence of the accuracy of the statements therein. Mr. 2962's second wife did not know him in 1943 when the reading was given. He met her later, and they were married in 1948. However, the characteristics ascribed to 2962 in the reading must have been definite ones for her to remember and associate with him *thirty-three years later*!

Cayce's story of Atlantis is derived from the set of life readings. It is difficult for me, as an engineer, to present the story. I can scarcely swallow the tale myself, even though I was a member of the family, had both physical and life readings, and listened to many of those for others. I can only tell you that the evidence for the accuracy of the physical readings is incontrovertible. Too many reports exist from patients and doctors who followed the suggested treatments and got good results. This evidence is on file in the A.R.E. library in Virginia Beach and open to public scrutiny. I know many of the life readings also proved helpful in the lives of those who requested them. It seems reasonable to suppose that there was some degree of accuracy in them also.

This does not prove that the Atlantean life readings are true. But evidence uncovered in recent years regarding past earth changes, climatic changes, pole reversals, and the migration of people in prehistoric times points to the accuracy of the readings rather than their falsehood. Edgar Cayce's fascinating story of Atlantis is at least worthy of serious consideration.

Edgar Evans Cayce

PREFACE

THE NAME "ATLANTIS" conjures up images of a mysterious civilization in the ancient past. Thousands of books have been written about this land; some try to prove it as fact, others try to dismiss it as fiction. In this book our approach is different. In it you will become acquainted with a remarkable psychic, Edgar Cayce, and his material on Atlantis. But we balance the psychic material with a scientific look at Cayce's accuracy. Was he right or wrong? Can we ever know for sure whether Atlantis existed?

This book looks at the legend of Atlantis in its many forms: from Plato, who first wrote of Atlantis; to scholars, who tried to prove Plato was right; to occultists, who made the entire legend suspect; and to skeptics, who tried to prove it never existed at all. We have pieced together Edgar Cayce's tale of Atlantis from over seven hundred "psychic readings" given over a twenty-one-year period. Cayce's account begins with humankind's arrival on earth some ten million years ago, and ends with the sinking of the last remnants of Atlantis around 10,000 B.C.

When the readings were given, Atlantis was in the realm of the occult, and science gave little credence to this type of information. Science is still largely unwilling to take psychic information seriously, and in many cases this is quite justified. But it is certainly possible to evaluate psychic material in comparison to scientific findings. We will look at geological and archaeological discoveries that have bearing on the Cayce story, from the time the first Atlantis reading was given in 1923 to the present day. New research techniques, not available when Cayce's readings were given, make it possible to now evaluate many of his readings. Some statements Cayce made in readings years ago, which sounded ludicrous at the time, have become part of mainstream scientific thought; others are still controversial but are being carefully studied by some researchers. Some of his predictions of future geological catastrophes are taken seriously indeed by geologists today.

A unique aspect of the Cayce work are the expeditions sponsored by the Edgar Cayce Foundation to search for the records of Atlantis—from the Sphinx of Egypt to the island of Bimini in the Bahamas. For the first time, this book tells the story of these expeditions and their findings.

We believe you will come away from this book with a greater appreciation of the potential for psychic information to contribute to our knowledge of the world. The Cayce readings did not encourage blind acceptance, but emphasized the value of testing the concepts and seeking proofs and facts. A reading in 1927, for a man who was publishing articles on the Cayce readings, stated, ''Present them and watch the fur fly . . . These will bring many in favor and many in disfavor—but what is needed most of mankind is to think! This will make one think!'' (no. 195–43, July 19, 1927).

This book is our invitation to you to think—about the scientific evidence, and about the implications of the story for your own life. You will discover a new view of human history on earth and what we can expect from the future.

MYSTERIES OF
ATLANTIS
REVISITED

Part I

STORIES OF ATLANTIS

1

THE LEGEND OF ATLANTIS

ATLANTIS—ONGOING SEARCH for "lost civilization" debated. So read a headline in the April 23, 1987, edition of the *Virginian-Pilot* newspaper. The article was about a symposium on the lost continent, sponsored by Atlantic University and the Edgar Cayce Foundation of Virginia Beach. The speakers ranged from skeptics to ardent believers: explorers who were convinced of the authenticity of the controversial finds of the 1960s and 1970s near the island of Bimini; researchers who felt that some of the sites might simply be natural formations; and archaeologists who were unconvinced by the evidence for Atlantis, but eager to encourage careful exploration without destruction of sites. For many, the symposium signaled the resurgence of interest in the story of Atlantis, a legend that simply won't go away. The evidence—sometimes striking, but often ambiguous—continues to come in, despite the best efforts of skeptics to relegate it to the realm of fiction.

To most people, the name "Atlantis" evokes an image of a land, somewhere in the Atlantic Ocean, that sank beneath the waves in ancient times. A host of questions naturally arise:

- Where did the story of Atlantis originate?
- Why is it called the "lost continent"?
- Is there any evidence such a place ever existed?
- Why is anyone still searching for it?

The *Encyclopaedia Britannica* describes Atlantis as follows:

> Atlantis—A legendary island in the Atlantic Ocean.
> Plato in the *Timaeus* describes how Egyptian priests, in
> conversation with Solon, represented the island as a
> country larger than Asia Minor with Libya, situated just
> beyond the Pillars of Hercules. Beyond it lay an archi-
> pelago of lesser islands. Atlantis had been a powerful
> kingdom 9000 years before the birth of Solon and its
> armies had overrun the Mediterranean lands, when Ath-
> ens alone had resisted. Finally the seas overwhelmed
> Atlantis, and shoals marked the spot. In the *Critias* Plato
> adds a history of the ideal commonwealth of Atlantis. It
> is impossible to decide how far this legend is due to
> Plato's invention, and how far it is based on facts of
> which no record remains.

The Pillars of Hercules were made up of the rock of Gibraltar (which was known as Calpo or Alybe in ancient times)
and Abyla, a hill in Africa, on the opposite side of the Strait
of Gibraltar, near Ceuta. These two landmarks overlooked the
entrance from the known world bordering the Mediterranean
into the unknown world of the Atlantic Ocean.

According to Plato, the information Solon received from the
Egyptian priests said that Atlantis, a continent-sized island in
the Atlantic, had been swallowed up by the sea in a violent,
volcanic catastrophe some 9,000 years earlier. Plato lived from
428 to 348 B.C.; Solon lived approximately 200 years before
Plato's time. This would place Atlantis in the Atlantic about
9600 B.C.

Are there earlier references to Atlantis? Hesiod, a Greek
poet who lived in the eighth century B.C., mentions the "Isles
of Blest" or "Fortunate Isles." They have become part of
Greek mythology and were located in the "western ocean"
(that is, the Atlantic). They were said to be peopled by mortals
upon whom the gods had conferred immortality and who enjoyed perpetual summer and abundance.

An even earlier reference to Atlantis may have been made
by Homer (whose era is estimated at anywhere from 850 B.C.

to 1200 B.C.), who speaks of the Phaecian land in his *Odyssey*. Unfortunately, Homer didn't give the exact location of this "Phaecian land."

Opponents of the Atlantis story question why there are no Egyptian records of the country. Proponents counter by speculating that references to it may have been lost when the library at Alexandria was burned.

Medieval writers, who heard Plato's tale from Arabian geographers, believed it to be true. They already had other traditions of legendary islands in the western sea. The Portuguese, for example, had the island of Antilia (or Antillia, Island of the Seven Cities), which was shown on a globe made at Nuremberg, Germany, in 1492. The geographer, Martin Behaim, relates that when the Moors conquered Spain and Portugal in A.D. 714, the island of Antilia was colonized by Christian refugees. Perhaps the word "Antilia" can be traced back to the Latin "anterior," or the island reached before Cipango (Japan), or even Atlantis. There is a Welsh legend of Avalon, a kingdom of the dead; and a Cornish legend of Lyonnesse, a legendary island off the coast of England that disappeared into the sea. The French have a legend of Isle Verte, and the Portuguese of an Ilha Verde. St. Brendan's Island and other legends of lost islands have been the subject of many sagas in various languages and were even marked on charts and became objects of voyages of discovery until the eighteenth century.

Literally thousands of books, articles, and pamphlets have been written about Atlantis. A few years ago the Association for Research and Enlightenment (A.R.E.) acquired the Egerton Sykes collection of books about Atlantis. They fill the four walls of an eight-foot-square room from floor to ceiling. To list the titles of all of them would require a volume the size of this one.

The writers range from scientists and amateur archaeologists to psychics and occultists. Some writers amass evidence to show that Plato's story was probable as well as possible. Others try to rationalize it by moving the location and changing the date to a more recent time. Still others consider the tale nothing but a myth, and collect data to prove their point.

THE MANY STORIES OF ATLANTIS

Donnelly's Version

The most widely read book about Atlantis is undoubtedly Ignatius Donnelly's *Atlantis, the Antediluvian World*. First published in 1882, it was revised by Egerton Sykes in 1949 and is still in print. Donnelly was well read. During his long tenure as a senator from Minnesota, he thoroughly explored the collections of the Library of Congress. He collected a tremendous amount of legendary, geological, and archaeological material to support his ideas. His arguments in support of Plato's tale can be persuasive indeed. William Gladstone, prime minister of Great Britain, was so enthusiastic about Donnelly's book that he asked the Parliament to approve funds for a ship to search the Atlantic for remains of the continent. But skeptics challenged both Donnelly's sources and his reasoning, and began a debate that continues today.

Donnelly set out to prove that Atlantis was a continent-sized island which once existed in the Atlantic. He was convinced that Plato's tale was not a fable, but based on reality. He believed that Atlantis was the cradle of civilization, where human beings rose from barbarism. In his mind, the kings, queens, and heroes of Atlantis were the gods and goddesses of Greek, Phoenician, Hindu, and Scandinavian myths. The acts attributed to them in mythology were actually a confused recollection of historical events.

To Donnelly, Atlantis represented a universal memory of a great land and was the basis for the stories of the Garden of Eden, the Garden of Hesperides, Mount Olympus, and other traditional locations where humankind once lived in peace and happiness. The inhabitants of Atlantis once carried on trade with Egypt, Africa, North and South America, Scandinavia, and countries bordering the Mediterranean Sea. Atlanteans were sun-worshipers and spread their religion as far east as Egypt and as far west as Peru. Because Egypt was Atlantis's oldest colony, its civilization resembled that of Atlantis.

Donnelly's imagination became stronger with each idea. He concluded that Atlanteans were the first people to manufacture bronze and iron, and that their alphabet was the forerunner of both the Phoenician alphabets and the Mayan glyphs. The original home of the Aryan or Indo-European family of nations, as well as that of the Semitic people, must have been Atlantis. Finally, he concluded that after Atlantis was destroyed in a terrible cataclysm, the survivors went both east and west, carrying with them tales of the catastrophe, which survived in legends of a flood.

Donnelly reasoned that Plato's account is based on fact, because his Atlantean history begins not with gods and demons, but with people who built temples, ships, and canals, and who traded and warred with surrounding countries. Because Plato was a renowned philosopher, Donnelly concluded that he would not descend to fiction.

Donnelly points out that geologists agree that the earth's surface was much different in the past. Many lands, once above the oceans, are now underwater, and lands once submerged are now above the seas. What they can't agree on is the time it takes for such events to occur. Geologists think in terms of thousands and millions of years, not such a short span as narrated by Plato.

Certainly, earthquakes and volcanic eruptions can happen quickly. For example on May 18, 1980, Mount St. Helens in southwestern Washington, just 40 miles north of Portland, Oregon, erupted. In an explosion seldom witnessed by people, one and one-half cubic miles of mountain were pulverized. The explosion was equivalent to 500 atom bombs the size of the one that destroyed Hiroshima. A cloud of dust, ash, and gas rose 63,000 feet above the earth and obscured the sun. Over 1,200 feet of the mountaintop was blown away. Snow and ice on the slopes melted, and the resulting landslide of mud and rocks wiped out Spirit Lake, filling it with debris. Mud and silt were carried as far as the Columbia River, and by the next day its normal 40-foot channel was silted up to 18 feet.

Of course this was a local disaster. Except for news reports, and the spectacular sunsets caused by dust in the atmosphere, inhabitants of the central states and east coast were relatively unaware that anything had happened. Geologists believe most such volcanic eruptions and earthquakes are local and cannot conceive of an event that would cause a continent to sink.

Some argue that a collision or near-collision with an asteroid or comet might cause widespread earth changes; but they also point out that such an occurrence is unlikely.

Speaking of the similarities of the flora and fauna, Donnelly quotes authorities of his day: "When the plants and animals of the Old and New Worlds are compared one cannot but be struck by their identity. Nearly all belong to the same genera while many, even of the same species, are common to both continents. This is important in its bearing on our theory that they radiated from a common center after the Glacial Period."

Donnelly points out that an examination of the fossil beds of the Miocene Age in Switzerland reveals the remains of over 800 species, the majority of which have migrated to America. Unless there was a land bridge between Europe and North America, or unless people were there to carry them, how could they travel between the two continents? He cites the banana or plantain found in Asia and Africa and cultivated in America before Columbus. It is seedless, with only a perennial root. People must have carried it across the sea. Donnelly thinks the plantain or banana was cultivated in Atlantis and carried both east and west, for a cultivated plant that does not possess seeds must have been under cultivation for a very long time. He says it is improbable that two countries on opposite sides of the ocean would have cultivated the same plant for that length of time. But the plantain isn't the only example. Donnelly quotes authorities as saying that certain roses, the tuberose, the lilac, and certain cereals—wheat, oats, rye, barley, and maize—have been under cultivation so long that they are not known in their wild state. Furthermore, their origin is unknown. He looks to Atlantis as the origin of these plants.

Turning next to customs, Donnelly produces a long list of similar practices on both sides of the ocean that indicate a common center of origin. For example, he says the practice of smoking tobacco prevailed among the Indians of both North and South America before Europeans arrived. Natives of certain parts of Africa use pipes also to smoke hemp and tobacco, and the use of pipes for smoking hashish and opium was prevalent from China to Arabia. He cites countless other customs common to Peruvians and early Europeans. For example, they both worshiped the sun and the moon, believed in human immortality and the resurrection of the body, and embalmed their dead. On both sides of the Atlantic, people examined the entrails of sacrificial people and animals, and had vestal virgins who were buried alive if they broke their vows. Other common practices included a twelve-month year, enumeration by tens, the existence of castes, and the passing of the occupation of the father to the son. Donnelly covers pages with other comparisons. He argues that so many similar customs could not have originated on both sides of the ocean independently.

Returning to Plato, Donnelly notes that the philosopher refers to a passage beyond the islands of Atlantis to other islands and the continent beyond, which surrounds the real sea. He calls the Atlantic a real sea as opposed to the Mediterranean, which is a landlocked body of water like a harbor. But the Greeks had made no sea voyages to America, so how did Plato know of this? The word Atlantic and the word Atlas are not from any language known in Europe. There is an Atlas mountain on the western shore of Africa (known from most ancient time) and an Atlan town on the eastern shore of America. The Aztecs claim to be from Aztlan. Even in mythology a mythical being, Atlas, holds the world on his shoulders.

Donnelly tries to tie in Greek myths with Atlantis, saying that the ancient Greek gods and goddesses were the kings and queens of Atlantis. He points out that the Egyptian historian Manetho refers to a period of 13,900 years as the reign of the gods.

He concludes by summarizing the cultural similarities on both sides of the Atlantic as proof that they originated from a common center. He makes a point of the fact that the Basques of the Pyrenees differ from their neighbors in appearance and language.

Donnelly's forceful style, learning, and enthusiasm tend to sweep the reader along and encourage overlooking of flaws later critics have found in his logic. In spite of his ingenuity and eloquence, his detractors claim he reasons from a "molecule of fact to a mountain of surmise." They also point out that some of Donnelly's sources were incorrect and led him to erroneous conclusions. For example, Basque is the only non-Aryan tongue of western Europe, but it is not similar to North American Indian languages, as Donnelly claimed. Much of Donnelly's discussion of the Mayan civilization is based on the work of a French scholar, the Abbé Brasseur de Bourbourg. Brasseur attempted to translate one of the three surviving Mayan manuscripts, the *Troano Codex*, based on the Mayan "alphabet" of Bishop Diego de Landa, who had been responsible for burning all the other Mayan books. With de Landa's bogus alphabet, and Brasseur's lack of linguistic expertise, the resulting "translation" was worthless. It is now known that the *Troano Codex* is a treatise on astrology, not a description of volcanic eruptions. Donnelly and his contemporary, the explorer Augustus LePlongeon, took Brasseur's translation seriously, and incorporated such statements as "One-third of the Mayan language is pure Greek" into their stories of Atlantis.

Spence's Version

After Donnelly, many other writers continued to accumulate evidence for the existence of Atlantis. Between 1924 and 1928, Lewis Spence produced three books: *The Problem of Atlantis, The History of Atlantis*, and *Atlantis in America*. The first is best, in that Spence's arguments and style are more scientific. He claims that there is enough evidence from geology, biology, and prehistoric European and South American cultures to conclude that Atlantis is a probability. He concludes that Plato was indeed describing facts and not making up a story in the *Timaeus* and *Critias*. Spence's second book, *The History of Atlantis*, involves more speculation than logical analysis, and endeavors to tie in Greek myths with Atlantis. His third effort, *Atlantis in America*, tries to show that Atlantis formed a land bridge between Europe and South America. He speculates that Cro-Magnon man may have gotten from Atlantis to Europe using that route. The book goes on to cite similar customs and legends of the Native Americans of North and South America and the natives of Egypt and Africa.

Bramwell's Version

James Bramwell wrote *Lost Atlantis* in 1937. He believes that Plato's account is only half-truths—a core of fact surrounded by imaginary and irrelevant material. He points out the errors of other writers on Atlantis, but also summarizes some arguments for the continent, one being the Cro-Magnon invasion of Europe 25,000 years ago. Cro-Magnon was a 6-foot, 6-inch-tall specimen with a high forehead, prominent cheekbones, and a firm chin, whose skull capacity was above that of modern human beings. Yet no one knows where this race originated. There was another invasion by a similar race 16,000 years ago and a third invasion by a race known as the Azilians about 10,000 years ago, close to Plato's date for the sinking of Atlantis. Bramwell's book features good criticism of the poor reasoning used by other authors in their efforts to prove the existence of Atlantis, along with a few bits of evidence that it may actually have existed. He ends his book on the note that Atlantis is probably a myth.

Berlitz's Version

In 1969, Charles Berlitz reviewed the arguments for Atlantis in *The Mystery of Atlantis*, and added some discoveries of his own. One of the most striking illustrations in his book is a comparison of what looks like a form of hieroglyphs, taken from Easter Island in the Pacific, with a sample from the Indus Valley in Pakistan. Neither has been deciphered, but the similarity of the two is so great that it is difficult to believe they do not have a common origin. In 1984, Berlitz updated his Atlantis material with the publication of *Atlantis, the Eighth Continent*. His evidence appears impressive; yet, as we shall see in a later chapter, there are many sides to the story, and quite a lot of skepticism about some of the new discoveries.

For a quick and impartial summary, Roy Stemman's *Atlantis and the Lost Lands* should appeal to almost any reader. This work, published in 1977, is one of the more recent ones. He maintains a neutral point of view, and condenses the arguments of a few of the most popular writers, both for and against the idea of a mid-Atlantic continent. He even includes the occultists. He mentions the results of recent dredging and coring samples taken from deep ocean waters: limestone and continental granite samples indicated that portions of the bottom have been above the surface in the past. His work is filled with colorful photographs and fanciful illustrations. For example, he provides photographs of the formation of the island of Surtsey, 20 miles southwest of Iceland, which was formed by volcanic eruptions between 1963 and 1966. A few pages later, there is an imaginative drawing of a Lemurian as described by W. Scott-Elliott, a well-known occultist. Photographs of the massive stone statues of Easter Island appear next to an artist's conception of an Atlantean aircraft.

THE OCCULTISTS DISCOVER ATLANTIS

The Atlantis story thus far—that of Plato, Donnelly, and others—was based on scholarship. This scholarship, although challenged by the establishment, was nevertheless based on written records, empirical evidence, and reasoned speculation. The "occult" tradition departs from this scholarly approach. It relies on "secret" teachings available only to "initiates."

Cayce's method was direct clairvoyant perception of metaphysical records. Yet, although some of the terms used by Cayce were popular among the occultists of his day, the Cayce readings often disagree with many specifics of the occult tradition. Cayce appears to have been far more accurate when compared with current scientific thought. However, because many people requesting readings were familiar with the contemporary occult teachings, Cayce may have sought to explain their past lives with concepts they could understand.

What did "occult" mean to someone seeking a reading from Edgar Cayce? The word *occult* can conjure up negative images for many, from witchcraft to voodoo. In the context of Cayce and this work, however, occult has a far different meaning. It refers to a tradition of secret teachings, passed down through the ages by initiates who have been trained in clairvoyant perception, which present a more accurate understanding of the nature of reality than that offered by either traditional religion or recent scientific theories. The most popular occult system in Cayce's time was Theosophy, founded in the late 1800s by Helena P. Blavatsky. These occult teachings are in part derived from Eastern religions, including Buddhism and Hinduism, and have an elaborate world plan of multiple planes of existence, and successions of "Root Races" of humankind. In the occult tradition, mystical experience plays a key role, and clairvoyant revelations continually enlarge and enhance the material.

The occultists did not reject the scholarly works on Atlantis, but instead used them as a jumping-off point. Their goal was far more lofty than simply explaining why languages or buildings are similar on both sides of the Atlantic. They wanted to understand the descent of humankind from its spiritual origins into the physical world. The Cayce material is closely allied to these traditions in the minds of many, for he too sought to explain the relation of the spiritual to the physical.

The basis of the occultist approach is that there are sources of information not limited by time and space. Rudolf Steiner, an outstanding occultist as well as one of the foremost scholars in Europe, pointed out that history can tell us very little concerning humanity in prehistoric times. Even geology and archaeology are limited by the physical evidence that remains. Those who have the capacity for clairvoyant perception of the spiritual world can report on events to which historians have no access. The skeptics would say that all this material was the product of overactive imaginations, yet these ideas have captured the interest of many scholars, and are not simply a popular fad. Steiner admits that spiritual seeing is not infallible; its vision may be inexact, distorted, or even the reverse of the actual case. But Steiner felt that people who have achieved a certain level of spirituality will receive consistent information. The question our book tries to answer is whether Cayce's material was simply imagination, or whether he tapped some source that allowed him to see a record of past events.

What did the Cayce readings have to say about the occultists? Cayce himself was not a member of any of these groups, and was not familiar with their doctrines; but some of his followers were. In the first discourse on the general topic of Atlantis, the readings said, "As we recognize, there has been considerable given respecting such a lost continent by those such as the writer of Two Planets, or Atlantis—or Poseidia and Lemuria—that has been published through some of the Theosophical literature. As to whether this information is true or not, depends upon the credence individuals give to this class of information'' (no. 364–1, February 3, 1932).

Thus Cayce acknowledged some of the popular occultist books, such as the book *A Dweller on Two Planets*, but warned his listeners that they should be careful about which occult material they took seriously. The terms used by Cayce, such as Akashic Records, Atlantis, and Lemuria, are also terms used by the occultists. Where Cayce differs is in his relation of ancient history to the past lives of individual people. All occultists paint an elaborate picture of Atlantis and the evolution of human consciousness, but Cayce adds the story of individuals and their personal development.

The following summary of the occult view of Atlantis approximates what Cayce's contemporaries had heard. Don't confuse it with the Cayce story, but take it as historical background. In many cases, Cayce modified or contradicted it.

The Theosophists' Version

Helena P. Blavatsky, the founder of Theosophy, wrote about Atlantis in her major work, *The Secret Doctrine*. Blavatsky claimed to have learned the doctrine from comparative study of the world's occult traditions during her extensive travels. *The Secret Doctrine* consists of excerpts from the *Book of Dzyan*, which she claimed to be an ancient book of wisdom, together with comments on her translation. Her detractors, such as writer L. Sprague de Camp, are dubious about the authenticity of the *Book of Dzyan*, and accuse her of plagiarizing it from various Eastern philosophical works. She may also have simply received the book clairvoyantly. Whatever its origin, *The Secret Doctrine* had a major influence on the course of thought about the spiritual evolution of humankind.

The goal of the Theosophical viewpoint is to explain the origin and evolution of the universe and the origin and evolution of humankind. Atlantis plays a significant role. Theosophy views seven as a mystic number: there are seven planes of existence, sevenfold cycles through which everything evolves, and seven Root Races of humankind. It is these Root Races, and especially the fourth or Atlantean, which concern us here. Since "Root Race" was a term used in the Cayce readings in a very different way, it is important to clarify the Theosophical concept.

The Theosophical saga describes the descent of the human spirit into matter, followed by upward evolution. Root Races do not correspond to our usual concept of race, or even of humanity. The Root Races begin with the first, the Polarean. The Polarean Root Race existed only in astral body form in the "Imperishable Sacred Land," not in physical matter. The second Root Race, the Hyperborean, dwelt in the Arctic continent of Hyperborea, a hypothetical continent in Greek mythology located in the far north. Hyperboreans had physical bodies, but with strong ties to the ethereal. They did not resemble what we think of as people, and were not normally visible.

With the third Root Race, the Lemurians, the Theosophical story begins to tie in with the scholarly thought of the late 1800s, and to provide a background for the Cayce readings. Lemurs, an animal related to the monkey, have an unusual distribution in the world. German biologist Ernst Haeckel noted that lemurs abound on the island of Madagascar, and are also found in Africa, India, and on some islands of the Malay archipelago. He speculated that a land bridge might have existed at some time connecting these lands and allowing free migration of the lemurs. Haeckel went on to suggest that this now-sunken land bridge may have been the original home of humankind. Darwinian evolutionary theory was becoming popular, and geologists had noted striking resemblances between rock formations in India and South Africa. The name Lemuria was suggested in an orthodox scientific context by British zoologist Philip Sclater for this hypothetical land bridge in the Indian Ocean between India and Madagascar. The idea of Lemuria was one of the first pieces of evidence leading to the theory of continental drift, which is now widely accepted. At that time, however, it was one of many theories attempting to explain the distribution of ancient geological formations and fossil animals.

The Theosophists freely acknowledge that they had taken Sclater's term to describe their own much broader concept. The Theosophical Lemuria, a much larger area than that proposed by Haeckel and Sclater, was a great southern continent occupying much of Africa, Asia, the Indian Ocean, and portions of the Pacific Ocean. The story of the Lemurians described human descent into physical matter. Lemurian "man" was regarded as an animal destined to reach humanity, rather than as human. According to Theosophist W. Scott-Elliott, the early Lemurians had gigantic gelatinous bodies, which began to solidify in the middle of the Lemurian period. These later Lemurians were between 12 and 15 feet tall, had no foreheads, had eyes set far apart so that they could see sideways as well as in front, and had an eye in the back of the head. Many were even less human in appearance than this.

Scott-Elliott's Version

With the appearance of the fourth Root Race, the Atlanteans, the Theosophical story became more complex. W. Scott-Elliott was the Theosophist whose work most directly relates to the Cayce Atlantis. Scott-Elliott first published *The Story of Atlantis* in 1896; but it was his expanded book, *The Story of Atlantis and The Lost Lemuria*, published in 1925, which some of Cayce's audience had probably read.

The Scott-Elliott material was also received clairvoyantly, and followed the standard Theosophical line of seven Root Races. He goes into elaborate detail regarding the Root Races and subraces. Scott-Elliott also provides detailed maps and specific dates for the destructions of Atlantis.

Scott-Elliott's Atlantis story covers about 5 million years of history, with four major destructions. The first catastrophe was 800,000 years ago. The maps show Atlantis as occupying most of the Atlantic Ocean. Some 200,000 years ago, most of Atlantis disappeared, leaving two large islands in the Atlantic, which Scott-Elliott named Ruta and Daitya. Notably, in contrast with the Cayce material, the Bahamas were not part of the Theosophical Atlantis. The third destruction occurred 80,000 years ago, and left only the island of Poseidonis, centered in what are now the Azores islands in the mid-Atlantic. Finally, the fourth destruction occurred in 9564 B.C. Scott-Elliott gives this exact date, and provides other dates as well. He says that the first migration to Egypt took place

400,000 years ago, and that there were Peruvian Incas 14,000 years ago.

Scott-Elliott's dates disagree with Cayce's; and, as we shall see later, Cayce's dates are far more reasonable in the light of modern scientific knowledge. Nevertheless, Cayce's description of Atlantis was more closely allied to occult thought than to the scientific thought of his time. Scott-Elliott repeats many of the speculations of the late 1800s, which scientists had proved wrong by 1925—among them that the Basque language of Europe had a resemblance to North American Indian languages; that Mayan writing is similar to Egyptian hieroglyphics; and, following LePlongeon, that one-third of the Mayan tongue is pure Greek. Cayce included none of this misinformation in his readings.

Churchward's Version

Before we leave the occultists, we must mention James Churchward and Mu. Mu was the name of a land that LePlongeon derived from a bogus translation of the Mayan *Troano Codex*. It is now known that the *Troano Codex* is primarily astrological and calendrical; but in the late 1800s, this translation telling of the ancient land of Mu was as reasonable as many interpretations of Mayan writing. Churchward expanded greatly on the story of Mu in a series of volumes published in the 1920s and 1930s. Mu, not then confused with Lemuria, once occupied most of the Pacific Ocean.

Although Churchward claimed to have translated documents, there is no evidence that the documents existed, and he is best classed with the occultists. By the time of the Cayce life readings, Mu and Lemuria were sometimes used interchangeably by occultists to refer to a continent in the Pacific Ocean, and Cayce uses the terms this way himself in a few life readings.

Cayce Versus the Occultists

What are we to make of this elaborate occult history, and how does it relate to the Cayce story? The occultists, like Cayce, received much of their material in clairvoyant trances. A Theosophist listening to Cayce might at first have thought his material to be just another expansion on the basic Theosophist story. Yet, beyond use of some of the same terms, the Cayce story bears little resemblance to the occultist story. A small amount of occult material did appear to be incorporated in the Cayce material. Whether this was because they were both tapping the same source, or because Cayce was picking up material from his audience, we have no way of knowing. The occultists, however, were the first to mention high technology, such as flying machines, in conjunction with Atlantis. Cayce later followed this theme in many life readings. Likewise, the occultists were the first to refer to multiple destructions of Atlantis, although Cayce disagreed with the dates and the number of destructions.

On the other hand, Cayce speaks of Lemuria, but only in passing; he speaks of the other Root Races not at all. There is no sign of the seven subraces of Atlantis. Cayce uses the term ''Root Race,'' but to refer to five entirely human stocks in different parts of the world. As the Theosophists used current scientific terms to convey their concepts, Cayce used Theosophical terms for his listeners. But to equate the Cayce concepts with Theosophy or any other occult doctrine is to misread Cayce. The readings are not a rehash of earlier work, but appear to build from that work to make concepts clearer to those who were steeped in the occult lore of the day.

THE SKEPTICAL RESPONSE

The skeptical books on Atlantis, while fewer in number, are entertaining and often present the facts more accurately. In *Voyage to Atlantis*, Dr. James Mavor gives the impression that he used the title and the legend to draw attention to his discovery of a possible sunken city in the Aegean Sea. To do this, he argues that Plato was wrong about the location of Atlantis and the date of its demise. He attempts to link Atlantis to a Minoan city on the island of Thera. Like Atlantis, it boasted a high civilization and was destroyed by an earthquake and volcanic eruption. However, its destruction took place about 1500 B.C.

In *Another Look at Atlantis*, Willy Ley begins by attacking the origin of the story, arguing that not all of Plato's colleagues believed him. He says that Aristotle (Plato's pupil) implied that the Atlantis story was fiction; that Strabo, the geographer, was noncommittal; and that when Pliny the Elder mentioned Atlantis, he added, "as far as we can believe Plato." Ley goes on to agree with Mavor that Plato must have been wrong about both the date and location of Atlantis. He thinks it is probable that the civilization Plato referred to was the Minoan civilization on the island of Thera that was destroyed by a volcanic eruption in 1500 B.C.

L. Sprague de Camp's *Lost Continents* is perhaps the most exhaustive critique of the various Atlantis stories. It follows the same line as Willy Ley, contending that Plato's story was just that—a story. He insists that people have always longed for a land of beauty and plenty where peace and justice reigned and, failing to find one in reality, created imaginary Edens and Utopias. He attacks the Plato story by saying that there is no mention of Atlantis, other than Plato's, in either Greek or Egyptian literature, but admits that it is possible that records of it may have been lost or destroyed.

De Camp accuses Donnelly of hasty and uncritical judgment. He argues that common beliefs are worldwide, and the fact that customs are similar on both sides of the Atlantic proves nothing. He says it is not true that Peruvian Indians had a system of writing; and that, although cotton plants are found on both sides of the ocean, they are of different species. He thinks it is possible to trace Egyptian culture from primitive people up to the highly acclaimed Fourth Dynasty. To refute Spence, de Camp claims that remains of Cro-Magnon man have been found in Palestine and that they may have come from the east instead of the west.

Donnelly compared the names of cities in Asia Minor and Central America, such as Chol and Chol-ula, Colua and Coluacan, Zuivana and Zuivan, Cholina and Colina, and Zalissa and Xalisco. He said that cities with such similar names on both sides of the Atlantic must imply some connection. De Camp disagrees, saying that one cannot take similar sounding words, such as the English *water* and the German *Wasser*, or *dix* in French and *disi* in Hottentot (both meaning "ten"), to prove languages are related. He says because there are only twenty to fifty phonemes (sound units) and several thousand words in any language, many will inevitably resemble one another. De Camp also says there are more differences than similarities between Old World and New World plants, and no relation between Egyptian and Mayan hieroglyphs.

He pokes fun at the occultists and Theosophists who have written so prolifically about Atlantis, and doesn't think anyone can take the story seriously. He does admit that what Plato meant by "the ocean and continent beyond Atlantis" is not clear to this day.

Anthropologist Robert Wauchope is another dissenter and the author of *Lost Tribes and Sunken Continents*. He regrets that most professional anthropologists do not write books that are popular with the average reader. He says that the preference is for sensational journalism, or the writings of mystics who tell of lost tribes and lost continents. He worries that many unwary readers will be persuaded that research is a process of manipulating and mixing facts with intuition and imagination. Contrary to his comments on most anthropologists, Wauchope writes with skill and humor. It is worth reading his book to understand the skepticism with which the majority of scholars view anything remotely connected with the word Atlantis. Wauchope concludes that the Atlantis legend is a myth.

We have the believers and the skeptics, the scientists and the occultists, yet there is no conclusion to the conventional tale. These references approach Atlantis from myriad angles, but none of them can help us answer the question of whether the Cayce material offers a perspective that may resolve the controversy.

EDGAR CAYCE ON ATLANTIS

The final reference to Atlantis—*Edgar Cayce on Atlantis*—was published in 1968. It grew out of Edgar Evans Cayce's efforts to delve into the 700 Cayce life readings that mention individual incarnations in Atlantis, and the influence of these past lives on the individual's present life. Clearly, if the place never existed, many of the life readings would be suspect. But Cayce mentioned Atlantis frequently, particularly in connection with its final destruction and the migration of Atlantean refugees to Egypt, the Pyrenees, and South and Central America. Some of these fleeing people, he said, carried with them records of their lost homeland. The discovery of any such records would certainly lend proof of the existence of Atlantis and validate Cayce's story of this lost continent.

Cayce described the development of civilization from the time human beings appeared on earth (over 10 million years ago, according to Cayce) to around 10,000 B.C., when the last remnants of Atlantis sank into the Atlantic. Edgar Evans Cayce correlated archaeological discoveries that had been made up to 1968 with statements from the readings. In 1968, however, we knew far less about the relevant archaeology than we know now. Archaeological and geological discoveries made in the last twenty years since the publication of *Edgar Cayce on Atlantis* tend to render many of Cayce's statements more probable. These discoveries are treated in later chapters. Now, however, let's take a look at Edgar Cayce's story of Atlantis.

2

EDGAR CAYCE'S STORY
OF ATLANTIS

TODAY I SPIT a mile.''

This slightly irreverent statement is attributed to a small boy who once stood at Bright Angel Point on the south rim of the Grand Canyon and gazed down at the Colorado River a mile below. For a look into the past, one can scarcely do better than visit Grand Canyon National Park. This immense gorge, cut by the Colorado River in the high plateau of northern Arizona, is truly a window in time. The scale of the canyon is enormous. It varies in width from 4 to 18 miles. From Bright Angel Point, one has a magnificent view of the Colorado River, a mile below. Within the canyon itself are a multitude of peaks, buttes, plateaus, ravines, gulches, and smaller canyons. Several different types of climate prevail at its different levels.

In the walls and rocks of the canyon, we can read a record of the past that extends back millions of years. Here are the windblown sands of a desert; here are shells, corals, and traces of marine life from long-forgotten shallow seas; here are remnants of plants and aquatic life from a former freshwater lake. The record of eons past goes back from the surface to the black basalt, exposed at the river. A trip down the canyon trail will convince the most skeptical that geologists' views of earth's long history are based more on hard evidence than on mere speculation.

Edgar Cayce traveled deep into the past as well. Rather than reading the story of the earth in the rocks, he read the Akashic Records, described in his readings as a psychic record of every event that has ever taken place, ''woven upon the skein of time and space.'' Geologists can only look at layers of rock and the fossil skeletons of ancient animals; but Cayce's journey into the Akashic Records revealed a vast wealth of information, including the past lives of many individuals.

Scattered through those hundreds of life readings is the tale of a once-great continent that attained a level of culture and technology unmatched in history. The readings also relate how this great society—in the struggle between people devoted to God and those devoted to material desires—destroyed all that they had as a result of their moral struggle and misuse of technology.

Cayce's readings agree with geologists that the surface of the earth was much different in the past. Many lands have disappeared, reappeared, and disappeared again. But the readings go beyond accepted geological theory, and geology can tell us nothing about the people themselves, how they lived, how they died, and what meaning their lives might have for us today.

We will look here at Cayce's description of Atlantis as pieced together from his journeys through time. The chapter is organized chronologically, beginning with the entrance of human beings onto the physical plane 10 million years ago, and ending with the final migrations from Atlantis.

This story presents a very different view of the past than that accepted by science in Cayce's time. It challenged the scientific view by speaking of great catastrophes, as recently as 10,000 B.C., in which islands and even an entire continent sank beneath the sea. Yet it did not simply follow Plato or the occultists. The Cayce story tells of multiple Atlantean catastrophes that occurred at intervals over a span of 40,000 years, not destruction in a single day and night, as narrated by Plato. Like Donnelly, the Cayce readings speak of migrations throughout the world, yet the Cayce description of the result of these migrations goes far beyond Donnelly. The Cayce Atlantis, with its high technological achievements and great moral conflicts, resembles the world of today more than the orthodox concept of the ancient world, or even the world of Cayce's day.

What makes the Atlantis readings special? Like all life readings, they were given to help individuals understand and answer the questions and problems they might have in their present lifetimes. In the case of people with past incarnations in Atlantis, the problems have a special urgency, both for the people themselves and the world at large. According to Cayce, many people who lived in Atlantis were active, influential, and capable individuals. These Atlanteans are incarnating again into the world today. Because their influence on world civilization was so great in the past, it is likely they may once again greatly influence world events.

Cayce expressed that thought this way: "Be it true that there is the fact of reincarnation, and that souls that once occupied such an environ [Atlantis] are entering the earth's sphere and inhabiting individuals in the present, is it any wonder that— if they made such alterations in the affairs of the earth in their day, as to bring destruction upon themselves—if they are entering now, they might make changes in the affairs of peoples and individuals in the present?" (no. 364–1, February 3, 1932). And elsewhere: "We meet few people by chance, but all are opportunities in one experience or another. We are due them or they are due us certain considerations" (no. 3246–1, September 28, 1943).

If what Cayce said is true, many of our problems with others may be left over from some past experience. If they are not solved now, they may well return to haunt us in future incarnations. Carrying this thought a step farther, if many individuals who had incarnations in Atlantis are returning to earth now, they may be returning to the same problems that caused such turmoil in Atlantis.

It is not too difficult to draw parallels between the Atlantean civilization described by Edgar Cayce and that of the United States today. Both developed a highly technical society. Both were world powers, and both were plagued with racial or social problems. Both developed weaponry that, if misused, could destroy their own country and even affect world climate.

In Atlantis, the worst happened—not once, but on three different occasions, the last resulting in the final destruction and sinking of the country. It is little wonder that many of the life readings that gave Atlantean incarnations were filled with warnings to individuals about the misuse of their abilities. Individuals who had misused their talents once before might easily follow the path of least resistance and misuse them again.

Not everyone who lived in Atlantis was a "bad guy." Many of the incarnations there were depicted as ones where the individuals had "gained," as Cayce put it, or had improved their understanding of their relationship to God and others. Certainly one message of the life readings is that it is possible to live a constructive life under any circumstances.

If the idea of reincarnation disturbs you, Cayce's story of humankind's coming into being in Atlantis and the philosophy involved may disturb you even more. It will probably please neither the evolutionists nor the creationists, for it contains a little of both theories plus a host of other material that challenges the dogma of many disciplines. I do not ask that you change your beliefs, only that you read with an open mind, particularly in light of the discoveries made and the events that have transpired since these readings were given.

PIECING TOGETHER THE CAYCE STORY

In contrast to Plato, Donnelly, or even occultists like Steiner, Edgar Cayce wrote no books on Atlantis. We must piece the story together from the nearly 700 individual life readings, given over a twenty-year period, that mention one or more Atlantean incarnations. This set of readings comprises a little less than 30 percent of the approximately 2,500 life readings.

Weaving the Atlantis story together from the life readings is a formidable task for two reasons. First, most of the remarks about Atlantis, or any other country, were in the nature of asides. The readings gave reasons for an individual's urges, tendencies, and personal characteristics, and even mental and physical abilities and disabilities; but they did not describe at length the times and places in which the person lived.

Second, few dates were given for the time of any particular incarnation. Because incarnations in Atlantis extended far into prehistory, it was difficult to tell how long ago the incarnation occurred.

Admittedly, much of the story is sketchy. But in spite of

these problems, many readings contained remarks about the customs or the times, and a few gave specific dates. Many of the remarks are at odds with conventional thinking, many of them sound as fantastic as any science fiction story and just as unbelievable. As I (Edgar Evans Cayce) sifted through the kaleidoscope of lives, however, I was impressed by the *internal consistency* of the information. Here were readings given as much as twenty years apart, for different individuals, which agreed in minute detail. There were few contradictions between readings for the same or different individuals given years apart. Names for over 400 different people were given in the Atlantis reading, with no confusion.

Cayce recounts three major periods of earth changes involving volcanic eruptions, earthquakes, tidal waves, and sinking land occurring between 50,000 and 10,000 B.C.:

- The first occurred about 50,000 B.C., when a portion of the continent was destroyed.
- The second occurred around 28,000 B.C., when the remaining land was split into islands.
- The final destruction occurred around 10,000 B.C., when the last islands were submerged. (This is undoubtedly the destruction to which Plato referred.)

These were not the only earth changes that ever occurred in Atlantis; other dates were mentioned. However, it was in these three periods that major changes came about, the shape of the land area was changed, and large numbers of people were forced to flee or migrate to other lands.

To find out what Edgar Cayce had to say about Atlantis, we read each of the 700 readings that mentioned it. We copied out paragraphs referring to Atlantis, and attempted to arrange the data in chronological order. We ended up taking the three periods of catastrophic destruction, each of which was associated with a specific date, as highlights of Atlantean history and tried to associate the references we had accumulated to one of these periods. Cayce often referred to these periods as the first, second, or final period of turmoil or destruction. When a particular life reading stated that the person had lived in Atlantis "before the first destruction," or after the period of the second destruction, or that he or she had migrated to another country during the final destruction, it was possible to place that individual roughly in a time slot. Unfortunately, many readings did not mention one of the destructions, and it was thus impossible to fix the approximate time of that person's incarnation.

The 700 Atlantean readings are associated with these time periods as follows:

A.	Associated with first destruction, 50,000 B.C.	21
B.	Associated with second destruction, 28,000 B.C.	52
C.	Associated with final destruction, 10,000 B.C.	352
D.	Of indeterminate date	275
	TOTAL	700

Table 2-1

Based on the general descriptions of situations and customs, we believe the majority of the readings listed as "of indeterminate date" fall somewhere in the period between 50,000 and 10,000 B.C., with the majority falling near the more recent date.

Cayce did not mention every incarnation an individual had experienced, but only those that had the most influence on his present life. In most life readings, previous lives were spaced out several hundred years going back from the present. Generally, Atlantean incarnations were the oldest, and some individuals had two or more incarnations in Atlantis. It seems probable that more recent lives would have more effect on an individual's present one than a life lived many thousands of years ago, because the person would have had time to work out many problems. Table 2-1 indicates that the vast majority of Atlantean incarnations, said by Cayce to have an influence on the person's present life, occurred around 10,000 B.C. One other factor that may have contributed to this lopsided distribution is the fact that Edgar Cayce himself had an incarnation in Egypt around 10,000 B.C., and many Atlanteans migrated there to escape the sinking of the last islands. Because they were associated with Cayce then, they were drawn to him in this life and obtained both physical and life readings, which in turn influenced the statistics.

In addition to readings on Atlantis's three periods of destruction, other readings push not only the age of Atlantis, but the age of humankind far, far back into the past. Not all of these readings are life readings of incarnations in Atlantis. Some were given in answer to general questions about the history of the mythical land; others dealt with the nature of human beings and our relationship to God and others. The reason for including data from such readings in a chapter on Atlantis is that, according to Cayce, Atlantis was one of the places where human beings first appeared on the earth. It was the place where human beings made their most rapid advancement toward what we consider civilization, and it was the place where the problems people created for themselves came into the sharpest focus. Chapter one explained how the Cayce readings spoke to many of the interests of the occultists of his day. A skeptic might imagine that Cayce brought up the topic of Atlantis in response to a popular fad. When the story of Atlantis is pieced together from the readings, however, it is clear that Cayce's story was not an idea that arose as a fad in one particular year. Table 2-2 shows the distribution of Atlantean life readings over a twenty-year span.

The column in Table 2-2 does not total 700, because it only includes individual life readings and not the general readings on Atlantis. The no. 364 series of thirteen readings, given in response to a request for a general lecture on Atlantis in 1932, would add to the total for that year. The distribution probably follows that of all life readings and of all readings of all types. For example, 1927 and 1928 were "lean" years, in that not many readings of any kind were given in those years. The interesting thing to me about the readings Cayce gave for twenty-one years is that statements made twenty years apart agree with each other. This is true of the information he gave concerning the nature and first appearance of humankind on earth, as well as material that described conditions in Atlantis at various times in its history.

Year of Reading	Number of life readings given that year in which Atlantis was mentioned
1923	2
1924	7
1925	14
1926	10
1927	6
1928	5
1929	10
1930	21
1931	17
1932	7
1933	25
1934	35
1935	45
1936	42
1937	35
1938	48
1939	66
1940	66
1941	58
1942	35
1943	64
1944	54
Total	672

Table 2-2

THE COMING OF MAN

When and where did human beings originate? The Atlantis story begins in the far distant past. Geology tells us of the skeletons of human beings and their relatives, yet the Cayce story is far more complex. Cayce describes our spiritual origin, our descent to the physical plane, and our gradual evolution to an awareness of our true spiritual nature.

What were the earliest dates mentioned in the readings? I found two readings that gave dates of 10 million and more years ago:

In the land now known as Utah or Nevada, when the first peoples were separated into groups as families . . . The entity [entity, sometimes called soul entity, refers to the soul or spirit, that part of an individual which Cayce said survives death] developed much and gave much to the people who were to succeed in that land, and in the ruins as are found in the mounds and caves in the northwestern portion of New Mexico may be seen some of the drawings the entity made. Some ten million years ago. (no. 2665–2, July 17, 1925)

In giving such in an understandable manner to man of today, it is necessary that the conditions of the earth's surface and the position of man in the earth's plane be understood, for the change has come often since this age of man's earthly indwelling. Many lands have disappeared, many have reappeared and disappeared again and again during these periods. At that time, only the lands now known as the Sahara, Tibet, Mongolia, Caucasia, and Norway appeared in Asia and Europe; that of the southern Cordilleras and Peru in the southwestern hemisphere and the plane of [present] Utah, Arizona, Mexico in the northwestern hemisphere.

The man's indwelling was then in the Sahara and the upper Nile regions, the waters then entering the now Atlantic from the Nile region rather than flowing northward; the waters in the Tibet and Caucasian regions entering the North Sea; those in Mongolia entering the Pacific; those in the plateau entering the Northern Seas. . . . (no. 5748–1, May 28, 1925)

The number of human souls then in the earth plane being 133,000,000. . . . The period in the world's existence from the present time being 10,500,000 years ago. When man came in the earth plane as lord of that in that

sphere, man appeared in five places then at once—the
five senses, the five reasons, the five spheres, the five
developments, the five nations. (no. 5748–2, May 28,
1925)

Sixty years ago, human history was measured in thousands
of years. To suggest that human beings, or even humanoid
creatures, lived 10 million years ago brought scornful laughter.
Since then, thinking has changed. New discoveries have rolled
back the dawn of humankind millions of years into the past.
In a later chapter, we will examine these discoveries in more
detail and compare them with specific statements in the Cayce
readings. For now, it is sufficient to note that recent scientific
discoveries, rather than typically disproving the readings, often
tend to render them more probable.

Were these "people," as we think of them now? The Cayce
scenario of 10 million years ago was far from the accepted
scientific opinion in his time, but is a mild heresy compared
to his readings that describe humanity's arrival on earth. Cayce
spoke first of projections by "thought forms" rather than
physical beings: "When there were those developments
wherein individuals were able to bring into being that as would
be called in the present through thought" (no. 2906–1, September 19, 1931). ". . . Understanding much as to the changes
that were wrought through the changing from the thought form
to the various associations with the material things of that
period" (no. 268–3, February 15, 1933).

Very few life readings refer specifically to incarnations in
this ancient period. Of the few that do, the remarks are strange
indeed. One reading states, ". . . the entity was in the Atlantean land and in those periods before Adam was in the earth.
The entity was among those who were then thought projections, and the physical being had the union of sex in one
body . . ." (no. 5056–1, May 6, 1944).

What do these statements mean? What is a thought form?
Was not Adam the first man, according to the Bible?

Probably the best way to explain what the readings are
talking about is to quote from a pamphlet originally compiled
by Hugh Lynn Cayce in 1935. *The Coming of Man* was
based on the no. 364 series of readings, the only readings

given by Edgar Cayce directly in response to a request for a lecture on Atlantis. He begins his article with a quotation from the Bible:

> Then God said, ''let us make man in our image, after our likeness; and let them have dominion over the fish of the sea, and over the birds of the air, and over the cattle, and over all the earth, and over every creeping thing that creeps upon the earth.'' So God created man in His own image, in the image of God He created him; male and female he created them (Genesis 1:26–27, KJV).

From the above, it is important that we grasp clearly one idea. Man was originally created in the image of the Creator. God was, and always will be, a Spiritual Being. When man first entered this plane, it was not in a physical form. He entered as a soul, a spiritual entity, in which there was embedded a spark of the Divine Fire. It was man, not God, who brought into existence the physical bodies in which the soul now lodges while on earth; it was man who gradually limited himself to the three-dimensional consciousness which is his present point of perception.

God created the earth just as one may create a beautiful thought. Each part, each element, sought only to magnify, glorify, the Creator. Peace and beauty reigned supreme in a harmonious expression of the Great Will. To this sphere, this strata of vibration, came one, Amilius, Son of the Most High, and with him came other souls, entities from other realms. In perfect accord with the laws already set in motion by the Creator, these entities truly enjoyed a spiritual life in a realm in which thought power controlled all things and the attributes of the soul found normal expression.

This was not the world which we see about us today; it was a world in attune with the Supreme will.

Amilius was endowed with a free will and the creative urge of the Father. He began to create companions, thought forms, patterned after the creatures given life by God. These thought forms were projections from the soul mind. As they began to seek gratification of the senses, as did the physical creatures about them, they began to harden and seek physical forms through which to become more conscious of the activity of the physical senses. We understand today that one actually becomes that which he takes into the system as food, that which he breathes and absorbs from the elements about him; in like manner one becomes that which he holds continually as mental visions. Incomplete and unbalanced, these resulting creations and mixtures brought discord and inharmony. The magnification of any desire which seeks only selfish gratification must eventually bring upon its creator anguish and final destruction.

The forms in the physical sense *were of the nature of thought forms*, able to push themselves out of themselves in that direction in which development took shape in thought—much in the manner of the amoeba in the water of a stagnant pool.

As these took form, by the gratifying of their own desire for that as builded, or added to, the material conditions, they hardened or set in bodies similar to those today, with a color partaking of the surrounding environ. There was the ability to project itself in whatever direction it chose. It was able to make itself of that environ, in color, in harmony, in whatever manner was desired. And this power resulted in projections in music, in art, in every conceivable manner; bringing all realms under subjection.

Through these thought forms man began to bind himself, for his selfishness turned upon him; he was, indeed, a Frankenstein. Chaos resulted. Peace and beauty fled before horror and misery. It was then that God created woman by dividing the spiritual being of man, thus creating a spiritual balance and preparing the way for a conquest of good over evil.

[Several readings indicate this with such phrases as the following: ". . . when there was the first division of sexes . . . among the first offspring of such division" (no. 2753–2, July 14, 1942) and "when there was the changing from double sex, or the abilities of propagation of activities from self'' (no. 2390–1, November 2, 1940).]

Amilius realized what was happening, realized that harmony had been overthrown through selfish gratification and abuse of creative power; so He took upon himself the burden of the world, the responsibility for the world. With the aid of entities who came to assist, He set about to conquer the self-projections which were more and more losing contact with God. From among the many physical shapes and sizes that resulted from the mixtures, He selected the form of the present man as the most suitable vehicle for physical manifestation on this planet. He then projected himself into five centers at once as Adam, the first man, choosing the five necessary expressions because of the five physical senses to be conquered before spiritual consciousness could be reached.

These five projections appeared simultaneously in five places on the earth. The white race appeared in the region of the Carpathian Mountains, the black race in the upper African region, the brown in Lemuria, the red in Atlantis, and the yellow in Gobi.

Thus Amilius, the first and last Adam, prepared the way for His conquest of the world, through man. Down through countless ages He has moved among men, sustaining them, ministering unto them, quelling their fears, ever urging them on. He has walked and talked with men of every clime, nurtured the seeds of every great religion that proclaimed the Oneness of God, fanned the fires of every great philosophy that pointed upward along the Way. In the hearts and minds of men He has kept alive the battle-cry for a conquest of self, and has, as an individual entity, led the way out of the great delusion which the inner man created and does create for himself.

This is an entirely different story of creation and humankind's arrival on the scene than that presented by either the theory of creationism or by evolution. It will probably satisfy neither. If the readings are true, then apparently people got into trouble very shortly after taking on material form. Problems arose almost immediately, as many of these beings used their new physical bodies for self-indulgence. These thought forms hardened into true physical bodies that parodied the animal life of that era, producing grotesque results. They may even have mixed with the animal life of that period. Some readings speak of humanoid creatures with animal attributes such as tails, feathers, fins, fur, scales, and hooves, even dwarfs and giants. Perhaps there is some substance to the old Greek myths of satyrs, centaurs, nymphs, and other strange creatures.

The more these souls succumbed to sensual pleasure by gratifying their own selfish desires at others' expense, the less able they became to move freely out of their physical bodies. At last they became trapped in them from birth to death, and many forgot or ignored their relationship to their Maker.

Cayce's readings for individuals bring the problems of Atlantis into sharper focus. He refers to specific groups and specific conflicts. A couple of quotations from Atlantean life readings refer to this early period before the first destruction of a portion of the continent: "In the Atlantean land when there were those disturbing forces—or just previous to the first disturbing forces that brought the first destruction in the continent, through the application of spiritual things for self-indulgence of material peoples. These were the periods as termed in the scripture when, 'the sons of God looked upon the daughters of men and saw them as being fair' " (no. 1406–1, July 13, 1937).

Six years later, another reading referred to the same problem: ". . . the entity was in Atlantis when there were those turmoils between the sons of Belial and the children of the Law of One. The entity was among the daughters of the children of the Law of One, and found the sons of Belial desirable for the material desires, for the gratification of material emotions" (no. 3376–2, November 22, 1943).

To quote Hugh Lynn Cayce again:

Very early in Atlantean history, two factions arose that were deeply split over the issue of how to treat these souls that had become so entangled in matter. The readings coined the terms of "sons of the law of one" and "sons of Belial." The sons of the law of one were those who believed the soul was a gift from God and strove to keep the race pure, free from animal characteristics and appendages. They wanted to aid those deeply entangled in the physical world and help them regain their positions as creatures of God. The sons of Belial were those without standard or morality and believed in gratification of the senses without respect to others. They looked down on these entangled souls as "things" to be treated as slaves or machines.

These "things," or souls who had pushed into matter without the consideration or ability of self-control, had become controlled by others and dependent upon others for direction and sustenance, much like a slave or house pet.

Such a state is exemplified by the following quote: "... a priest who ministered to the physical needs of the people. Thus those who were in that stage of development or awareness in which their minds and bodies only worked for others or performed the manual activities were of special interest to the entity; in attempting to use the spiritual forces to awaken the consciousness of those individuals to the point that they could raise themselves from those positions to that of greater relationship to the universal consciousness" (no. 2246–1, June 11, 1941).

It is important to understand how people developed in Atlantis, and to recognize the two factions that arose as a result. Individuals representing these two factions—the followers of the Law of One and the followers of Belial—warred with each other throughout their lifetimes. Many of these struggles must have gone on over long periods of time because some readings indicate that to live 500 to 700 years then was no more than to live 50 to 70 years today. Cayce seems to be echoing the fifth chapter of Genesis in which a number of men, including Methuselah, are reported to have lived very long lives.

According to Cayce, the people were extremists. Their talents properly used led to great advances spiritually and materially; but when misused they led to just as great regression spiritually and to self-gratification and strife physically.

Ever since that ancient time, people have been faced with choosing to develop an unselfish nature that longs for a return to a spiritual relationship with God; or succumbing to the selfish side that urges self-gratification, even at the expense of others, and maintains that the physical is all there is. It is not too difficult to draw a parallel between conditions then and conditions now: Consider the differences between the rich and poor nations of the earth; look at the race relations in South Africa and even in our own country.

The major problems facing the world today—our relationship to God and our relationship to each other—are not new. In Atlantis, these problems led to strife among the inhabitants of the land and finally to the destruction of the land itself.

THE FIRST DESTRUCTION

The first destruction of a portion of Atlantis appears to have been accidental; or to have been caused by explosives that got out of control and triggered volcanic action: ". . . with the continued disregard of those who were keeping the pure race and the pure peoples . . . man brought in destructive forces to be used by people that were rulers. These destructive forces combined with those natural resources of the gases, of the electrical forces made in nature, caused volcanic eruptions in the slow cooling earth, and that portion now near what would be termed the Sargasso Sea first went into the depths. With this there again came that egress of peoples" (no. 364–4; February 16, 1932).

Unfortunately, there is no simple chronology of events between 10,000,000 B.C. and 50,000 B.C., the next definite date in the Cayce readings. A few readings refer to a time "before the first destruction." Because 50,000 B.C. is given as the time of the first sinking of a portion of Atlantis, we assume that references to "before the first destruction" are to some period before this first sinking. How long before is anyone's guess. It may be a hundred, a thousand, or even a million years. We get the impression, because many of these references are to "just before" or "prior to," that the time frame is relatively close; that is, within a few hundred or at most a few thousand years.

Two extracts mention this period and the high technology that had developed since human entry to the physical plane: "In Atlantis before destructive forces arose—associated with communications . . . lighter-than-air machines . . . radio-active forces" (no. 1023–2, October 17, 1935). "In Atlantis before the first of the destructive forces . . . entity built those that made for the carrying those machines of destruction that sailed both through the air and under the water" (no. 1735–2, October 16, 1930).

Another clue to Atlantean technology, and its potential for misuse, comes from a reading given in 1941: ". . . in Atlantean land . . . just preceding the first breaking up of the land when there was the use of many of those influences that *are again being discovered* that the sons of Belial turned into destructive forces . . . intended for benefits to communications, transportation, etc." (no. 2560–1, May 8, 1941).

What could Cayce have been talking about when he spoke of influences just being discovered in 1941, which were powerful enough to cause the destruction of a country, yet could also have a beneficial use in communications and transportation? In 1940, scientists discovered that the fission in ordinary uranium did not come from U-238 but from the isotope U-235. In December 1942, the first sustained and controlled production of atomic energy was accomplished at the University of Chicago. If Cayce was right, this was not the first time human beings had control of a force powerful enough to be a blessing or a curse. Since 1941, the by-products of atomic energy development have been extremely useful. For example, many of the most up-to-date medical procedures are an outgrowth of this development.

The destruction of Atlantis apparently began with an effort to destroy a large number of animals, which had become a menace. The information in the readings is quite consistent. Here are eight references given in eight separate readings over a period of eighteen years that refer to the same event:

> . . . in that land where people came as representatives of those who would make the lands secure against the

beasts of the field and fowls of the air or animals of the air. (no. 2740–2, January 21, 1926)

. . . among those who came as messengers from foreign lands when people planned to protect themselves from beasts of the fields and fowls of the air. (no. 2675–4, April 15, 1926)

. . . in days when the peoples of nations gathered together to defend themselves against fowls of the air and beasts of the fields . . . came to meeting in lighter-than-air machine. (no. 2749–1, May 13, 1926)

. . . of that country to which messengers came when there was the gathering together of men to defend themselves against beasts of the field and fowls of the air. (no. 2855–1, May 29, 1926)

. . . in that land when there were gathering of nations to combat forces of the animal world and kingdom that made men and men's life miserable, entity among those that stood for use of elements in the air, the elements in the ocean, the elements in the lands as applied to forces to meet and to combat those of the animal kingdom. Oft has the entity, from this experience, been able to almost conceive wherein the disappearance of those known as prehistoric animals came about. (no. 2893–1, August 13, 1929)

. . . in Atlantean land during those periods when there were the first of the rebellions that brought the misapplication of the knowledge; or the forces that might have been used constructively but were used in destructive activities. The entity joined with sons of Belial who brought about destructive forces in the attempts to destroy the animal life that in other lands overran same. (no. 1378–1, June 1, 1937)

. . . when there was the meeting called from those of many lands to determine means and manners in which there would be control of the animals that were destructive to many lands. Entity in capacity of one who guided the ships that sailed both in the air and under the water, also was the maker of that which produced the elevators and connecting tubes that were used by compressed air and steam and the metals in their emanations . . . especially as to things controlled by the facet for the radiation activity of the sun on metals and control of such and airships. (no. 2157–1, March 27, 1940)

. . . in Indian land when Saad was ruler . . . among those who gathered to rid the earth of enormous animals which overran the earth but ice, nature, God changed the poles and the animals were destroyed, though man attempted it at the time. (no. 5249–1, June 12, 1944)

Could it have happened? We will see in the next chapter that Cayce's mention of a pole shift and climate change allows us to take a scientific look at the readings. In any case, this was clearly one of the major events near the time of the first destruction.

Cayce made repeated references to a world meeting and an animal menace. In a special reading, he was asked about the gathering. He replied,

In the period when this became necessary, there was the consciousness raised in the minds of the groups, in the various portions of the earth, much in the manner as would be illustrated by an all-world broadcast in the present day of a menace in any one particular point, or in many particular points. And the gathering of those that heeded, as would be the scientific minds of the present day, in devising ways and means of doing away with that particular kind or class of menace.

As to the manner in which these gathered, it was very much as if the Graf [Graf Zeppelin?] were to start to the various lands to pick up representatives, or those who were to gather, or were to cooperate in that effort. And as this then was in that land which has long since lost its identity, except in the inner thought or visions of those that have returned or are returning in the present sphere, the ways and means devised were as those that should alter or change the environs which those beasts needed, or that necessary for their sustenance in the particular portions of the sphere or earth that they occupied at the time. And this was administered much in the same way or manner as if there were sent out from various central plants that which is termed in the present the death ray or the super-cosmic ray, that will be found in the next 25 years. . . . [The] date B.C. of this gathering [was] 50,722. (no. 262–39, February 21, 1933)

It is interesting to ponder Cayce's reference to the death ray, and the statement that it would be discovered in the next twenty-five years—that is, by 1958. In 1958, three engineers at Bell Telephone Laboratories succeeded in constructing and operating a MASER, the forerunner of the laser. Of course, since then, the uses of masers and lasers have become widespread in communications, medicine, and many other fields. The use of a laser as a death ray is classified, although it is an open secret that the military is working along these lines in the so-called "Star Wars" weapons. Three years earlier, in 1955, scientists discovered the antiproton. By 1957, they concluded that antimatter was a possibility. Were antimatter to come in contact with ordinary matter, the resulting explosion would be many times greater than that from a fission or fusion reaction (that is, an atomic or hydrogen bomb). Certainly the term "death ray" could be applied to either of these discoveries.

Although many people perished in the first destruction and many migrated to other countries, Atlantean civilization was not totally destroyed. Readings covering the period from 50,000 B.C. to 28,000 B.C. speak of a continued high civilization. Incarnations for that period mention occupations that imply a high level of technology. Some people were said to have worked with machinery, electrical and chemical forces, radiation and heating, and mechanical appliances. Others were said to have worked in art and decorative work, or as ambassadors and diplomats. Still others worked with "crystals" that sound like modern lasers. Many readings imply the existence of atomic power plants and the ability to transmit power without wires. Remember, most of these readings were given long before the development of the atomic bomb, or the construction and use of atomic power plants and atomic-powered naval vesels. At that time, the use of the atom for power was considered implausible. Now its use is commonplace—many of our nation's utilities derive a large portion of their electrical power from atomic power plants.

We still consider it implausible that any civilization could have developed such technology many thousands of years ago. Technology, however, can develop very quickly. Less than fifty years ago, for example, the use of the atom for power or for bombs was unknown; the computer and the laser were science fiction. Jet planes, radar, and television stem only from World War II. We are now beginning to scratch the surface of genetic engineering and advances in superconductivity, which may revolutionize our science. All of this has occurred in less than a hundred years. The period from 50,000 B.C. to 28,000 B.C.—22,000 years—is longer than our recorded history: certainly a sufficient amount of time for considerable scientific advancement.

THE SECOND DESTRUCTION

Thousands of years after the first destruction, the land was once again plunged into turmoil, as the conflict between the children of the Law of One and the children of Belial continued. As always, the readings emphasized the influence of the past lives in Atlantis on opportunities in the present:

> . . . the entity was in that now known as the Atlantean land, during those periods of what is termed as the second change or upheavals, when there began those attempts of the sons of Belial and of the Law of One to instruct portions of the laymen, or those that were as laborers in those active fields of service in that particular land.
>
> The entity then was a priestess in the temple of the Law of One.
>
> Hence those things mechanical, yet things as pertain to electrical forces, things as pertain to cleansing— whether in that as would find an expression in nursing, teaching, ministering—will become and are a portion of the innate forces as find themselves in expression through the emotions of the body.

The tendency to submerge the emotions then must be overcome, *but directed*! (no. 1206–3, December 16, 1936)

Readings about the second destruction said the land was split into three principal islands and a few smaller ones. Cayce named these islands as "Poseida [Poseidia?] and Aryan and Og" (no. 364–6, February 17, 1932). Poseidia was frequently referred to as the major island remaining.

Fortunately, we have a date for this second period of destruction. To a question about an incarnation in Peru, Cayce replied,

As indicated from that just given, the entity was in Atlantis when there was the second period of disturbance—which would be some twenty-two thousand, five hundred [22,500] before the periods of the Egyptian activity covered by the Exodus; or it was some twenty-eight thousand [28,000] before Christ, see?

Then we had a period where the activities in the Atlantean land became more in provinces, or there were small channels through many of the lands.

And there were those, with the entity and its associates or companions, who left the activities to engage in the building up of the activities in the Peruvian land. For the Atlanteans were becoming decadent, or being broken up owing to the disputes between the children of the Law of One and the children of Belial. (no. 470–22, July 5, 1938)

A number of Atlanteans sought to escape the feuding between the followers of Belial and the followers of the Law of One. Some went west, to what is now Peru, the Yucatan, parts of Nevada, and Colorado. Others groups headed east to the Pyrenees and Egypt.

Technological development continued, and became a key element in the struggle between the children of the Law of One and the children of Belial. For example, ". . . in Atlantean land when there was the second division or when there was the destruction of the lands that made Poseidia the remaining portion in which there was the greater activity of the Sons of The Law of One. These periods when there was the application of much that is being discovered or rediscovered today, in application of power to modes of transit as well as use of nature's means for a helpful force in giving greater crops for individual consumption—period when a great deal of thought was given to conveniences of every kind" (no. 2562–1, May 9, 1941).

What kind of things could have been "rediscovered" or applied to modes of transit or greater crop yields in 1941? According to the *Encyclopaedia Britannica*: "In the mid 1930s the diesel engine began replacing the steam engine and by 1950 only a small fraction of new locomotives were steam powered." Also, "The war years [World War II] marked the beginning of the rapid growth of the use of the airplane in carrying commercial cargo." In a few years, U.S. air-cargo carriers were flying more than 100 million ton miles of freight and 80 million ton miles of express annually. Those years also marked the beginning of the use of the helicopter as a short range carrier.

As for agriculture, it was the beginning of farm mechanization. The use of tractors on farms increased from 250,000 a year in 1920 to more than 2 million in 1945. In terms of plant nutrients, the use of fertilizer and lime in 1944 was 85 percent above the quantity used between 1935 and 1939. The use of hybrid seeds added 400 million bushels to the corn crop in the early 1940s. The United States became the food arsenal of the United Nations.

I am not implying, by this analogy, that the Atlanteans used diesel engines or farm tractors. It would seem reasonable, in the light of their technological achievements, that they developed hybrid seeds and used fertilizers and lime to increase crop yields, and that they made comparable advances in transportation.

Numerous readings that describe this period of technological advancement contain scattered warnings to those who had the readings to be careful to use their abilities for good or constructive purposes rather than for bad or destructive reasons. For example: ". . . in the Atlantean land when there were activities that brought about the second upheaval in the land.

There the entity was rather the electrical engineer, as would be called in the present: For the entity applied those forces or influence for the directing of airplanes, ships, and what you would today call radio for destructive as well as for constructive purposes" (no. 1574–1, April 19, 1938).

The readings also continue to mention the conflict between the two factions, the sons of the Law of One and the followers of Belial. The principles of this conflict were established ages ago but continue to this day: ". . . in the Atlantean land during those periods when there were those determining as to whether there would be the application of the laws of the children of One or of the sons of Belial in turning into destructive channels those influences of infinite power as were being gained from the elements as well as from what is termed spiritual or supernatural powers in the present. Entity wavered between choices and when the destruction came about by the use of those rays as were applied for beneficial forces, entity misapplied ability—*hence the influence of atomic energies or electrical forces of any nature becomes a channel for good or bad today*" (no. 1792–2, February 11, 1939).

Another quote refers to an incarnation in which one woman helped those who wanted to lose their animal characteristics and develop a more perfect physical body. The time of this incarnation was given as "before the second destruction," which would place it before 28,000 B.C.: ". . . aided in the attempts to establish for those that were developing or incoming from the thought forms into physical manifestations to gain the concept of what their activities should be to develop toward a perfection in physical body, losing many of the appurtenances that made for hindrances" (no. 444–1, November 16, 1933).

The Firestone

It was during the period of the second destruction that Cayce, in describing the technological advancement of the Atlanteans, used the terms "Tuaoi stone," "firestone," and "crystals" to describe a power source. This power source was to become a key element of Atlantean civilization, and was eventually responsible for the destruction itself. Asked about the Tuaoi stone, Cayce replied,

> It was in the form of a six-sided figure, in which the light appeared as the means of communication between infinity and the finite; or the means whereby there were the communications with those forces from which the energies radiated, as of the center from which there were the radial activities guiding the various forms of transition or travel through those periods of activity of the Atlanteans.
>
> It was set as a crystal, though in quite a different form from that used there. Do not confuse the two then, for there were many generations of difference. It was in those periods when there was the directing of aeroplanes, or means of travel; though these in that time would travel in the air, or on the water, or under the water, just the same. Yet the force from which these were directed was in this central power station, or Tuaoi stone; which was as the beam upon which it acted.
>
> In the beginning it was the source from which there was the spiritual and mental contact. (no. 2072–10, July 22, 1940)

This excerpt seems to mean that originally the so-called Tuaoi stone or crystal was a means of communicating with the spiritual realm in the early days of Atlantean history, when people had begun to project into materiality. *Later* it became the term for any source from which great power radiated, and was then referred to as "firestone" or "terrible crystal."

Another reading, which gives a graphic description of the firestone or crystal, sounds to me like a layperson's attempt to describe a giant laser. Cayce was asked to "give an account of the electrical and mechanical knowledge of the entity as Asal Sine in Atlantis." As always, in his answer Cayce related past lives to opportunities for individuals in the present:

> Yes, we have the entity's activities during that experience. As indicated, the entity was associated with those that dealt with the mechanical appliances and their ap-

plication during the experience. And, as we find, it was a period when there was much that has not even been thought of as yet in the present experience.

About the firestone that was in the experience did the activities of the entity then make those applications that dealt with both the constructive and destructive forces in the period.

It would be well that there be given something of a description of this, that it may be better understood by the entity in the present, as to how both constructive and destructive forces were generated by the activity of this stone.

In the center of a building, that today would be said to have been lined with non-conductive metals, or non-conductive stone—something akin to asbestos, with the combined forces of bakelite or other non-conductors that are now being manufactured in England under a name that is well known to many of those that deal in such things.

The building above the stone was oval, or a dome wherein there could be or was the rolling back, so that the activity of the stone was received from the sun's rays, or from the stars; the concentrating of the energies that emanate from bodies that are on fire themselves— with the elements that are found and that are not found in the earth's atmosphere. The concentration through the prisms or glass, as would be called in the present, was in such a manner that it acted upon the instruments that were connected with the various modes of travel, through induction methods—that made much the character of control as the remote control through radio vibrations or directions would be in the present day; though the manner of the force that was impelled from the stone acted upon the motivating forces in the crafts themselves.

There was the preparation so that when the dome was rolled back there might be little or no hindrance in the application direct to the various crafts that were to be impelled through space, whether in the radius of the visioning of the one eye, as it might be called, or whether directed under water or under other elements or through other elements.

The preparation of this stone was in the hands only of the initiates at the time, and the entity was among those that directed the influences of the radiation that arose in the form of the rays that were invisible to the eye but that acted upon the stones themselves as set in the motivating forces—whether the aircraft that were lifted by the gases in the period or whether guiding the more pleasure vehicles that might pass along close to the earth, or what would be termed the crafts on the water or under the water.

These, then, were impelled by the concentrating of the rays from the stone that was centered in the middle of the power station, or power house (that would be termed in the present).

[This reading goes on to say that power stations of this sort were set up in various portions of Atlantis. Unintentionally, they were] . . . tuned too high—and brought the second period of destructive forces to the peoples in the land, and broke up the land into the isles. (no. 440–5, December 20, 1933)

This power source was also used for medical treatment, just as lasers today are used in certain forms of surgery: "Through the same form of fire the bodies of individuals were regenerated, by the burning—through the application of the rays from the stone, the influences that brought destructive forces to an animal organism. Hence the body rejuvenated itself often, and remained in that land until the eventual destruction" (no. 440–5, December 20, 1933).

Atlantis was not entirely destroyed in this second period of destruction. The readings imply that a series of volcanic eruptions, earthquakes, and flooding split the remaining land into islands. Another polar shift probably occurred, as some readings speak of a change in climate. An advanced civilization still remained, even though some of the technology may have been lost in the sinking of much of the land. The two factions survived this cataclysm and continued their feuding. One reading speaks of this period: ". . . in the Atlantean land during those periods between the second and the last upheavals; when there were the great antagonistic feelings between the sons of Belial and the children of the Law of One. The entity was among the children of the Law of One who made the greater overtures to those peoples for the acknowledging of the laborers, and to make their experiences easier—those laborers that were considered by many as merely *things* rather than individual souls" (no. 1744–1, November 12, 1938).

That some technology survived the second destruction of Atlantis also is evident from these following extracts: ". . . in Atlantean land when there were the attempts to reconstruct the activities of the people after the second of upheavals or breaking up of the land or continent . . . applied materially electricity or electrical forces" (no. 1861–2, November 23, 1939). And, ". . . in that land now known as the Atlantean during those days when there were the attempts of those to bring quiet, to bring order out of the chaos by the destructive forces that had made for eruptions in the land, that had divided the lands and had changed not only the temperate to a more torrid region but by the shifting of the activities of the earth itself" (no. 884–1, April 9, 1935).

There is little further information in the readings about the period from 28,000 B.C. to 10,000 B.C. Atlantean culture and technology, however, appear to have prospered.

THE FINAL DESTRUCTION

Most of the readings on Atlantis referred to the time of the final destruction. Like the readings that focused on the earlier periods, they described life situations in past incarnations which had an impact on the present. These lives help us to understand Atlantean culture at the time, and lead up to the final destruction and migrations to lands of safety.

These last Atlanteans had long since taken on human form. One reading describes an Atlantean at the time of the final destruction: "The Atlantean [378] five feet ten inches, weighing a hundred and sixty pounds; color as of *gold* that is burnished; yet keen of eye, gray in color. Hair as golden as the body. In activity alert, keen, piercing in vision, and of influence on those that approached'' (no. 275–38, February 16, 1934).

The people of Atlantis were as varied as people are today, some gaining in their experiences and some losing. In the 18,000 years between the second and final destructions, some science survived, as did the two factions, the sons of the Law of One and the sons of Belial. The following excerpts from the readings tell the stories of the people from Atlantis, and illustrate the diversity of lives at this time.

Some helped the oppressed and gained a great deal during this struggle: ''. . . the entity was in the Atlantean land, when there were those periods of the oppressions by the sons of Belial and the children of the Law of One, and those peoples in the lesser position of the laboring class. The entity assisted its companion then to stand for those that were being the greater taxed, the greater oppressed, those that were being given less and less privileges for the enjoyments of the associations of their own families, the associations of the fruits of their own labors'' (no. 1261–1, September 14, 1936).

Others gained through development of their special talents and coping with the difficult times during the final destruction: ''. . . the entity then one of the greater entertainers of the time, though not reaching any great height on account of the change in the ruler of the forces pertaining to entertainment of the peoples, during the change. In the development, the entity gained much, especially in the way of being amenable to conditions and able to work under any circumstance'' (no. 2665–2, July 17, 1925).

Another person was a priestess, who in that life focused on the physical aspects: ''. . . in that country now submerged, and the entity among those of the high priestesses . . . Loving pomp, loving glory, loving in the desires of being bounded about those things that gave ease, comfort, and feelings of earthly conditions; yet losing little in that experience'' (no. 37–1, August 2, 1927).

Between 11,000 B.C. and 10,000 B.C., whether from psychic perception or from an interpretation of natural events, the leaders of Atlantis came to realize that the remaining islands were about to break up and sink. The submergence of these last islands took place over a period of time, and many inhabitants were able to flee the country. This is not to say that the disappearance of the last bits of land was not violent or without the loss of life; but, according to Edgar Cayce, many Atlanteans escaped to other countries, carrying with them records of their homeland. This is illustrated by the following quotations from life readings:

> With the realization of the children of the Law of One that there was to be the final breaking up of the Poseidian-Atlantean lands, there were the emigrations, with many of the leaders, to the various lands. (no. 1007–3, June 26, 1938)
>
> . . . in the Atlantean land when there was the breaking up of the isles and it had been given out that those that would or were to be saved must journey to the various centers to which the leaders had been given the passports. The entity was among those that came first to what is now the Pyrenees and later to the activities, after they had been set up years before, in the Egyptian land. (no. 633–2, July 26, 1935)
>
> . . . in Atlantean lands during those periods when there were the activities that brought about the last destruction through the warring of the sons of the Law of One and the sons of Belial . . . among those sent to what later became the Yucatan land. (no. 1599–1, May 29, 1938)
>
> . . . in Atlantean land when there were those periods of the last upheavals or the disappearance of the isles of Poseidia . . . among those who went to what later became the Inca land. . . . the Peruvian land as called in the present. (no. 3611–1, December 31, 1943)

In most cases, details on the migrations are scattered through the life readings; but one general reading inquired into the origin and development of the Mayan civilization. The following extract from this reading is quoted because of its connection with Atlantis and the specific date.

From time as counted in the present we would turn back to 10,600 years before the Prince of Peace came into the land of promise, and find a civilization being disturbed by corruption from within to such measures that the elements join in bringing devastation to a stiff-necked and adulterous people.

With the second and third upheavals in Atlantis, there were individuals who left those lands and came to this particular portion then visible.

But understand, the surface was quite different from that which would be viewed in the present. For, rather than being a tropical area it was more of the temperate, and quite varied in the conditions and positions of the face of the areas themselves.

In following such a civilization as a historical presentation, it may be better understood by taking into consideration the activities of an individual or group—or their contribution to such a civilization. This of necessity, then, would not make for a complete historical fact, but rather the activities of an individual and the followers, or those that chose one of their own as leader.

Then, with the leavings of the civilization in Atlantis (in Poseidia, more specific), Iltar—with a group of followers that had been of the household of Atlan, the followers of the worship of the *One*—with some ten individuals—left this land Poseidia, and came westward, entering what would now be a portion of Yucatan. And there began, with the activities of the peoples there, the development into a civilization that rose much in the same manner as that which had been in the Atlantean land. Others left the land later. Others had left earlier. There had been the upheavals also from the land of Mu, or Lemuria, and these had their part in the changing, or there was the injection of their tenets in the varied portions of the land—which was much greater in extent until the final upheaval of Atlantis, or the islands that were later upheaved, when much of the contour of the land in Central America and Mexico was changed to that similar in outline to that which may be seen in the present. (no. 5750–1, November 12, 1933)

Some Atlanteans used their skills to build a new life during the migrations:

... the entity was in the Atlantean land, during the periods when there were many of the divisions that called for and produced the destructive forces in that land. Yet when there were the expressions of those in power to raise those who were of the menial class, or the workers in the fields of activity that brought what is known as the agricultural or the social service, the entity was the intermediator for the own peoples of the lower class or caste to those of the higher ...

... among those that went ... eventually to that known as the Yucatan and the Central American land; for in those sojourns the entity was active in establishing a development in the agricultural field, or the growth of those things that made for the sustenance in the new land. (no. 801–1, January 27, 1935)

A number of readings give incarnations in Egypt at the time of the last destruction of Atlantis. A good bit of material is included in these readings about Atlanteans coming into Egypt, and the records they brought with them. We will go into this story at length in chapter five, which discusses the Edgar Cayce Foundation's explorations in Egypt.

Although its technology may not have been as high as in past times, Atlantis still had an advanced civilization when the last islands disappeared into the sea. Communication and travel existed between Atlantis and other countries, such as India, Gobi, the Pyrenees, Peru, the Yucatan, parts of North America, and Egypt. One reading even mentioned Indochina and Siam (now Thailand). Vocations were as varied then as now; people were psychologists, chemists, teachers, and diplomats. A type of aircraft was still in use, and some type of electrical treatments were used in hospitals to remove "appendages" from those still bearing these animal characteristics. For example: "... in Poseidia before the final breaking up. ... controlled activities regarding communications with many lands and the flying boats that moved through the air or water were means whereby the entity carried many to the Iberian land, later to Egypt, when it had been determined the records were to be kept there ... found land in a turmoil ... later with return of priest joined with movements for the regeneration of the bodies of 'things' in that period. Again active in communications" (no. 3184–1, August 28, 1943).

Another reading specifically mentions the last destruction: ". . . conducted people from Atlantis to Egypt previous to the last destruction . . . worked with adorning buildings with gems and precious stones" (no. 955–1, July 20, 1935).

Another mentions the "complete destruction," which we can assume means the last: ". . . in Atlantis when there was rebellions by children of Belial . . . and preparations for leaving because of upheavals and influences that were to bring about the complete destruction . . . journeyed to what is now a part of Spain, later to the Egyptian land" (no. 2283–1, June 14, 1940).

The final destruction of the last islands, like the first two, may have included a polar shift and a climatic change along with the volcanic eruptions and earthquakes. Details are lacking, other than that the submergence of the land took place over a period of time and many of the inhabitants had time to go to other countries.

Cayce gave no exact date for the disappearance of the last island. People were said to have fled Atlantis as early as 10,500 B.C.; other dates nearer to 10,000 B.C. mention people fleeing to Egypt carrying records with them. The final disappearance was probably after 10,000 B.C., for the following reading—one of the first ever given mentioning Atlantis—gives an incarnation in Atlantis about 10,000 B.C.: "In the one before this, we find in that fair country of Alta or Poseidia proper . . . in the household of the ruler of that country . . . This was nearly 10,000 years before the Prince of Peace came" (no. 288–1, November 20, 1923).

The disappearance of the last islands marks the end of Atlantean history and the end of this chaper. Chapter five explores the possibility that records of Atlantis were buried in Egypt, and the Edgar Cayce Foundation's search for these records, as well as its efforts to date the Great Pyramid. Should such records ever be found, history would have to be rewritten.

How could such a technically advanced civilization have existed as recently as 12,000 years ago and as long as 50,000 years ago, and simply have vanished without a trace? Perhaps there are traces, and we haven't looked for them in the right places. Archaeological work is expensive and time consuming. It does not concern the public as much as who will win the World Series or the Super Bowl. It does not receive a fraction of the support our government gives the defense budget.

How could an advanced civilization vanish? Think a moment. The more technically advanced a civilization is, the easier it is to destroy. Suppose the United States were to sink into the sea. Suppose the survivors had to flee to remote areas, such as the headwaters of the Amazon, or the heart of Africa, where people live very primitively. The survivors could not take their four-wheel-drive trucks with them; there would be no roads and no fuel. Their radios and TVs would be useless without broadcasting stations. Without credit cards and supermarkets, the majority would have difficulty surviving the first year. Those who did survive would do so by adapting to a life very much like that of the natives of the land to which they came. After a few hundred years, only legends of their homeland would remain. After 12,000 years, it is unlikely that any trace of them could be found.

Before you close your mind to the possibility that an advanced civilization existed in the distant past, read the testimony of geology and archaeology in the next chapters and see how many of Cayce's statements (which seemed silly at the time they were given) have proved to be accurate. Look at the research that has been done so far to discover a record of Atlantis. See what avenues look promising for further discoveries. The facts may surprise you.

Part II

THE SCIENTIFIC VIEWPOINT

3
THE TESTIMONY OF GEOLOGY

ATLANTIS AS A continent is a legendary tale. . . . Recently, however, the subject has taken on greater import, since some scientists have declared that such a continent was not only a reasonable and plausible matter, but from evidences being gradually gathered was a very probable condition'' (no. 364–1, February 16, 1932).

Edgar Cayce began this reading in response to a request for a lecture on Atlantis. The readings he gave tied in with the many life readings, presenting a picture of geography, geology, and archaeology covering a period of over ten million years. Is there any scientific validity to the Cayce story of Atlantis?

As we saw in chapter one, a great deal has been written about Atlantis, ranging from the books of Ignatius Donnelly in the 1800s to the deluge of popular books in the 1970s. Unfortunately, while some of the statements in these books are based on the best scientific opinion of the time, others are based on unconfirmed hearsay. Many of these books perpetuate rumors first started in other Atlantis books without acknowledging the source or verifying their accuracy. All too frequently, stories of the Bermuda Triangle and UFOs are mixed in such a hodgepodge that it becomes difficult to tell fact from fiction. We follow a different course here. The actual scientific discoveries are often more exciting than the hearsay, and are surprisingly consistent with the Cayce readings. They offer the very real possibility that Atlantis may yet be found.

This chapter and the next one highlight scientific discoveries relevant to the readings, but they do not attempt to cover all areas in depth. That would take many volumes. But everything in these chapters is taken from the scientific literature, and references are provided so that you can conduct your own research if you are so inclined. This information is not necessarily the final truth, for many scientific finds and theories are modified by later discoveries, and scientific controversies can last for many years. But it does reflect the state of scientific opinion, both in Cayce's time and now. It shows how many of Cayce's statements that were considered ridiculous in his own time are now part of the accepted body of scientific knowledge. Other Cayce statements still do not fit the concepts of modern science; a few are counter to some major scientific theories; for others, there is not yet any compelling evidence for or against.

We will look at the direct evidence for and against Atlantis. Were parts of the Atlantic Ocean above water at the times given in the readings? Are there any ruins of a high civilization? We will also look at some of the indirect evidence. Were there catastrophic volcanic eruptions and floods? Is humankind as old as the readings said? Could North and South America have been peopled by refugees from Atlantis?

THE SCIENTIFIC WORLDVIEW IN CAYCE'S TIME

Since at least the time of the Bible, people have known that the world was far different in past ages. Fossil sea shells have been found high in the Alps, and oil from long-decayed tropical plants has been found submerged in the Arctic. The biblical explanation was that a huge catastrophe, the "flood," had wiped out most of the life on earth. Calculations in 1654 by the Irish Bishop Ussher, based on the genealogies in the Bible, placed the date of creation at 4004 B.C.—so whatever force was responsible for the huge changes in the earth must have been sudden and catastrophic.

In the 1800s, *catastrophism*, the idea that the earth had been shaped by ancient catastrophes, had become a part of main-

THE SCIENTIFIC VIEWPOINT 61

stream science. Baron Cuvier, the great French naturalist, published his *Theory of the Earth* in 1812, which interpreted the geological record in catastrophic terms. Cuvier felt that the surface of the globe had been subject to a "vast and sudden revolution," which buried the countries formerly inhabited by people, and had left the bottom of the former sea dry. This catastrophe was thought to have occurred not further back than five to six thousand years.

The principle of *uniformitarianism*, set forth in definitive form by the English geologist Charles Lyell in 1838 through his classic text *Elements of Geology*, was opposed to the views of Cuvier. Uniformitarianism holds that the earth's geological processes have been operating unchanged, and within the same range of rates, throughout the earth's history. These rates are the same observed today, and are clearly gradual in nature. One immediate conclusion from this principle is that the earth must be millions, not thousands, of years old in order for the observed changes to have taken place.

The debate raged throughout the nineteenth century. Even Charles Darwin, whose theory of evolution was inspired by Lyell's work, felt that some catastrophe must have been necessary to cause the simultaneous extinction of many species. By the twentieth century, however, the debate had largely been settled in favor of the idea of uniform geological processes.

Geologists believed that the world was millions of years old, but dates could only be calculated by estimating the rate of the current process. For example, a geologist could measure sedimentation in lake bottoms or erosion of river banks, and calculate how long it should have taken for a lake to fill with sediment or a deep canyon to be cut. The layers of sediments with fossils in them, corresponding to geologic ages, were given names, but the dating of these ages was still largely guesswork. Actual catastrophic processes would make dating impossible and were not considered.

This was the paradoxical situation in Cayce's time: catastrophes were considered crank science, but geologic dating was largely guesswork. Author Francis Hitching quotes Derek Ager, professor of geology at the University of Swansea in England as saying that "Catastrophism became a joke, and no geologist would dare postulate anything that might be termed a 'catastrophe' for fear of being laughed at.'' Thus Cayce's references to multiple catastrophes could not be taken seriously, and his specific dates were beyond the capacity of science to verify or refute.

CAYCE'S ANCIENT GEOGRAPHY

Exactly what did Cayce have to say about the ancient world that was so controversial? His Atlantis readings cover a period from 10.5 million years ago to about 12,000 years ago. They speak of vast, catastrophic changes: "Many lands have disappeared, many have appeared and disappeared again and again during these periods . . ." (no. 5748–2, May 28, 1925).

The readings describe a geography totally unlike that of today:

> . . . that now known as the Southern portions of South America and the Arctic or North Arctic regions, while those in what is now [known] as Siberia—or that as of Hudson Bay—was rather in the region of the tropics . . . (no. 364–4, February 16, 1932)
>
> The extreme northern portions were then the southern portions, or the polar regions were then turned to where they occupied more of the tropical and semi-tropical regions . . . the Nile entered into the Atlantic Ocean. What is now the Sahara was an inhabited land and very fertile. What is now the central portion of the country, or the Mississippi Basin, was then all in the ocean; only the plateau was existent, or the regions that are now portions of Nevada, Utah, and Arizona formed the greater part of what we know as the United States. That [land?] along the Atlantic [sea] board formed the outer portion then, or the lowlands of Atlantis. The Andean or the Pacific coast of South America occupied then the extreme western portion of Lemuria. (no. 364–13, A-6, November 17, 1932)

The Cayce statements apparently combine aspects of various theories of ancient geography and climate change; but their emphasis on catastrophes was far from the orthodox position of the day. The Cayce description of the world 10 million years ago appeared to be quite close to what was already known as the Late Cretaceous period, around 80 million years ago. Internally, however, the Cayce view of the world was quite consistent. In 1959, a geologist wrote a booklet for the A.R.E. called *Earth Changes*, which discussed the consistency of the Cayce picture of the ancient world. This was the first attempt by any scientist to make sense of the Cayce readings. He wished to remain anonymous, concerned that even showing interest in Cayce might damage his career.

The geologist showed that, if a globe is rotated to match the locations of the poles as described by Cayce, positions of the areas of the world mentioned in the readings are in reasonable positions for the climates attributed to them. The geographic position of the North Pole would be in the vicinity of 15 degrees south latitude and 40 degrees east longitude, or, very roughly, Mozambique. The geographic South Pole would be in the vicinity of 15 degrees north latitude and 140 degrees west longitude, or, roughly, some 1,300 miles east-southeast of the Hawaiian Islands.

Geologists of Cayce's time recognized that climates had been very different in the past, but had not yet arrived at a unifying theory to explain ancient geography. Some of the geological layers containing tropical plant and animal fossils were found in temperate areas. Many areas that had clearly once been under water were now part of mountain ranges. Some animals, such as the lemurs of Madagascar mentioned in chapter one, had an unusual distribution. This led geologists to posit ancient land bridges. Yet the geological picture in Cayce's time was far from complete; it could not settle the question of the existence of land bridges or lost continents.

The Revolution in Geological Theory

Since Cayce's death in 1945, the world has seen a revolution in our concepts of ancient geology. Our understanding of the movements of continents is now based on a theory once considered as unlikely as the Cayce scenario. The first step toward understanding modern geological arguments for and against

Atlantis is to understand a little about the theory of continental drift.

Alfred Wegener, in *The Origins of Continents and Oceans*, published in English in 1929, first proposed in detail the idea that the continents could drift and that Africa and South America once fitted together like pieces of a puzzle. Wegener was ridiculed for failing to explain what force would permit "continents of granite to plow through oceans of rock." Wegener's intuition was powerful; but, like Cayce's, it was not backed by solid scientific evidence in his own time.

Wegener would be pleased to know that the theory of continental drift is now the key to modern geology. It was not until the 1940s that the proofs needed for Wegener's theory began to be found. Sonar, developed in World War II, was used to map the mid-Atlantic ridge, considered since Donnelly to be a possible location for Atlantis. The geology of the mid-Atlantic ridge was unusual. The entire ridge, which runs from South America to the North Pole, seemed to be undergoing constant volcanic activity. It was extremely active geologically, and the seafloor actually seemed to be spreading apart. This could be the driving force for continental drift. The proof came from a study of the magnetic fields in the ancient undersea lava.

When molten lava hardens, the direction of the earth's magnetic field at the time of hardening becomes locked into the lava. It can be measured millions of years later. In the early 1960s, it was discovered that the magnetic poles had flipped many times in the last several million years. Measurements to either side of the mid-Atlantic ridge showed magnetic stripes, several miles wide, magnetized in alternating directions. This suggested that lava eruptions from the ridge were creating new seafloor, and that the seafloor was indeed spreading. By 1965, the idea that the seafloor could spread was accepted by geologists, and the new field of plate tectonics was born. The continents were conceived of as giant plates, moved by seafloor spreading that originated at the mid-ocean ridges. One of the better books describing these concepts is Walter Sullivan's *Continents in Motion*, a firsthand account of the expeditions that led to the acceptance of the concept of plate tectonics.

The New Technology of Prehistoric Dating

Since Cayce's death in 1945, the word has seen a revolution in the technology of prehistoric dating, which has completely upset the concepts held in the first part of this century. It is now possible to accurately date events going back many millions of years; this dating has shown that the earth is far older than even the uniformitarians would have predicted, and has confirmed that catastrophic change sometimes does occur.

Most of the techniques for prehistoric dating rely on measuring small amounts of radioactivity in samples of ancient material. Different elements emit radioactive particles at different rates, and are naturally transmuted to other elements over a very long period of time. By measuring the relative percentages of these radioactive elements, it is possible to determine the age of a sample.

For archaeology, over the period of time covered by the Cayce readings, the most useful technique has been Carbon-14 dating, invented by Willard Libby of the University of Chicago in the late 1940s. Carbon-14 is a radioactive isotope of carbon; radiocarbon dating consists of measuring the amount of Carbon-14 present in a once-living organism, in comparison with the amount of nonradioactive carbon. Radioactive carbon is created in the atmosphere as cosmic rays bombard nitrogen atoms. This radioactive carbon is taken in by plant life during photosynthesis and by animals that feed upon the plants. Upon the death of the organism, Carbon-14 intake ceases and the radioactive carbon present begins to decay back to nitrogen at a fixed rate. After a lapse of a specific period of time, the amount of radioactivity in a substance will be reduced to exactly one-half; after a lapse of an equal amount of time to one-fourth of its original level; and so on. The half-life of Carbon-14 is about 5,730 years, so this method allows dating back to about 40,000 years.

By measuring the amount of radioactivity left in animal bones, ancient plant material, and charcoal from fires left at ancient campsites, it has been possible to go beyond dating based on purely geological layers and get ''absolute'' dates as to when the animals or plants died. By noting the type of geological layer, inferences can be made as to the age of the same layer in other locations when there is no carbon present. Radiocarbon dating has sometimes been criticized, because it depends on the assumption that the amount of Carbon-14 has remained constant in the atmosphere through the ages. Fortunately, radiocarbon levels can be calibrated through tree-ring dating. Each year a living tree produces a layer of cells that can be seen in cross-section as a ring. By counting rings, it is possible to tell how old a tree is. The deserts of the American West and some other areas contain some extremely old trees, both standing and fallen. By measuring the radioactive carbon in the rings of the fallen trees, it is possible to calibrate the Carbon-14 scale. Results have shown that the technique is accurate to within about 10 percent.

Since the invention of Carbon-14 dating, many other methods of absolute dating have been developed, each most accurate with certain types of material over a certain range of years. For pottery, thermoluminescence dating, which is based on the luminescence caused by the firing of the pottery, has proved very useful in the same range covered by Carbon-14. For geological deposits, potassium-argon dating is useful for millions of years.

With the advent of these new theories and techniques, our interpretations of the geological and archaeological record began to change dramatically. What relevance does this have for Atlantis? First, now that the movements of the continents were better understood, evidence for the existence of Atlantis could be reexamined. Second, the discovery of magnetic polar reversals spawned a new line of research that was to confirm a major concept in the Cayce readings: the idea that the poles of the earth had shifted in the past, giving rise to the catastrophes which were to destroy Atlantis. Finally, the invention of techniques for prehistoric dating opened up the possibility of confirming or refuting Cayce's dates for these catastrophic events. Let's take a closer look at the Cayce Atlantis readings in the light of these new discoveries.

WAS CAYCE'S ANCIENT GEOGRAPHY CORRECT?

What have we learned since Cayce's time that could prove him right or wrong? Although the existence of Atlantis as a continent is still a matter of some controversy, the views of the readings on geography and geological processes are receiving more and more support. On the surface, Cayce's statements describe a world far different from that of today. The Sahara as a fertile land! The Nile running into the Atlantic Ocean! Yet skeptical opinions have frequently been formed more from lack of evidence than from any strong evidence against the Cayce concepts. The existence of Atlantis is still controversial; yet even one of Cayce's most unlikely statements, that the Nile once flowed into the Atlantic Ocean, has recently been confirmed using satellite radar and photography.

The Nile is an outstanding example of how rapidly scientific opinion can change when new evidence appears. The readings stated, "The man's indwelling was then in the Sahara and the upper Nile regions, the waters then entering the now Atlantic from the Nile region rather than flowing northward" (no. 5748–1, May 28, 1925). ". . . the Nile (or Nole, then) emptied into what is now the Atlantic Ocean, on the Congo end of the country" (no. 5748–6, A-15, July 13, 1925). ". . . this same land now called Egypt (this before the mountains rose in the south, and when the waters called the Nile then emptied into what is *now* the Atlantic Ocean" (no. 276–2, February 20, 1931).

The Cayce descriptions of the ancient Nile, including his dates of 10.5 million years ago (no. 5748–2, May 28, 1925), are now very close to the opinion of the scientific mainstream. In an article published in *Science* in August 1986, R. Kerr discussed how, using the Shuttle Imaging Radar in the Space Shuttle, scientists discovered a previously unseen network of river valleys beneath the driest part of the Sahara where Libya, Egypt, and the Sudan met. When sites along the rivers were excavated, the scientists found 250,000-year-old riverside campsites. The source of the river was the Red Sea Hills between the Red Sea and the present-day Nile, and the river flowed across the Sahara and into the Atlantic at the bottom of the bulge of west Africa, exactly where Cayce said. Cayce pinpointed the location of human habitation as the upper Nile regions (upper referring to the headwaters area), an area now confirmed as fertile.

The dates determined by the new findings are also consistent with the Cayce dates. Cayce spoke of the Nile flowing into the Atlantic 10.5 million years ago, and of later settlements in the area. The new discoveries have established that this ancient Nile probably existed up until almost six million years ago, when the *rise of mountains* changed its course and it cut its present valley toward the Mediterranean.

Did Atlantis Exist?

Science now offers some support for the concepts in the Cayce readings on the Nile; Atlantis, however, is considerably more problematic. The Nile was never a big issue, but much energy has been devoted to proving the existence or nonexistence of Atlantis. Where exactly did Cayce say Atlantis was located, and is there any geological evidence that it was actually there?

> The position as the continent Atlantis occupied, is that as between the Gulf of Mexico on the one hand—and the Mediterranean on the other . . . There are some protruding portions within this that must have at one time or another been a portion of this great continent. The British West Indies or the Bahamas, and a portion of same that may be seen in the present—if the geological survey would be made in some of these—especially, or notably, in Bimini and in the Gulf Stream through this vicinity, these may even yet be determined. (no. 364–3, February 16, 1932)
>
> [Q-3.] How large was Atlantis during the time of Amilius [the first Atlantean]?
> [A-3.] Comparison, that of Europe including Asia in Europe—not Asia, but Asia in Europe, see? This composed, as seen, in or after the first of the destructions, that which would be termed now—with the present position—the southernmost portion of same—islands as

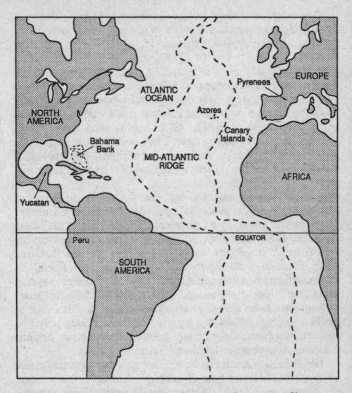

Figure 3-1. Map of Atlantic Ocean and surrounding continents, showing locations of possible sites for Atlantis and Atlantean migrations.

created by those of the first (as man would call) volcanic or eruptive forces brought into play in the destruction of same.

[Q-4.] Was Atlantis one large continent, or a group of large islands?

[A-4.] Would it not be well to read that just given? Why confuse in the questionings? As has been given, what would be considered one large continent until the first eruptions brought those changes . . . Then, with the breaking up, producing more of the nature of large islands . . . (no. 364-6, February 17, 1932)

What does this mean in terms of the geology of the Atlantic Ocean? Within the pattern of drift of the continents, was there ever room for a land mass larger than Europe? It is a difficult question. The geology of the Atlantic is not simple—different areas have different likelihoods of having been above water. Current geological theory finds it impossible to accept that the *entire* Atlantic Ocean was once a continent, but geologists have considered the possibility that certain areas of the ocean were once dry land.

Some of the argument about Atlantis hinges on the word "continent." In the theory of continental drift, continents are large granite masses, very different from the rock of the ocean floor. As the seafloor spread from volcanic eruptions on the mid-Atlantic ridge, the ocean bottom was formed from the lava. Thus, to a geologist, use of the word "continent" is inappropriate. A much better phrasing of the Atlantis question would be: "Could any area of what is now the Atlantic Ocean bottom have been above water within the last few thousand to million years?" When the question is asked in that way, the theoretical objections of many geologists go away. Atlantis becomes a subject for legitimate scientific inquiry.

The Atlantic Ocean can be divided into three general areas, each with a different type of geology: the mid-Atlantic ridge, the oceanic basins, and the continental margins. Each occupies roughly one-third the width of the ocean. The largest feature is the mid-Atlantic ridge, an underwater mountain range that extends like an elongated spine along the axis of the ocean. The ridge plays a major role in continental drift. It has been known since the last century, and was a major inspiration for Donnelly's theories of Atlantis.

The Cayce readings imply that Atlantis existed in all three areas of the Atlantic, but only the Bahama bank near the continental margin of North America was specified as a location where evidence would actually be found. We will consider all three areas, but Cayce's specific location has fared better than his general description. The question of whether the middle of the Atlantic Ocean was ever above water is still debated by geologists, but it is generally agreed that the Bahama bank was above water. As we will see in chapter six, explorers have made controversial discoveries of underwater formations that could be Atlantean ruins.

First, however, we will look for a lost continent in the middle of the Atlantic Ocean. The mid-Atlantic ridge is a mountain range, consisting of parallel ridges separated by valleys 20 to 30 miles wide. The mountains bordering these rift valleys descend on both sides into deep oceanic basins through several terraces. A number of ridges run across from the mid-Atlantic ridge toward the continents—for example, the Azores-Gibraltar ridge. Robert Ballard, the discoverer of the wreck of the *Titanic*, has published an atlas of the ridge and rift valleys that shows the rugged underwater territory. Its steep cliffs, deep canyons, and mountains would be a greater challenge to mountain climbers than any on land.

Many geologists have commented on the possibility of a sunken Atlantis on the mid-Atlantic ridge, but their opinions have generally been based on very little real information. As early as 1949, geologist Maurice Ewing, who became one of the fathers of the new geological theories, published a short article in the April 1949 *Science Digest* titled, "Lost Continent Called Myth." He is quoted as saying he has "mapped, probed, sounded, and visited the ocean depths since 1935." He took undersea photographs along the mid-Atlantic ridge as deep as 18,000 feet and "found no evidence of buried cities." Now, of course, nearly forty more years of exploration have taken place. Even though they may not be sympathetic to Atlantis, few geologists would feel that Ewing had performed a thorough survey.

With all the geological survey work that has been done, the ridge is still one of the most likely places to find evidence of a sunken civilization; yet such evidence has been hard to confirm. In most cases, the tops of these mountains rise to less than two miles below sea level, but some are currently islands. Some have flat summits, and contain coral reefs and shallow-water sediments, suggesting that they were once near the surface. In the late 1970s, the Soviets announced that they had found the ruins of Atlantis. According to an article by Oleg

Sulkin in *Soviet Life* in September 1980, the Soviet research vessel *Moskovsky Universitet* took underwater photographs on the Ampere seamount of what appeared to be giant staircases. Interpretations of the photographs varied from Atlantean ruins to natural formations. A year later, Dr. Andrei Aksyonov, deputy director of the Shirsov Institute of Oceanography, announced to the press (in an Associated Press story in the *Virginian-Pilot* on Friday, June 26, 1981) that more recent photographs were now believed to be of natural formations, and that the search for Atlantis in this area had been discontinued. Considering the catastrophic destruction of Atlantis, it may be too much to hope for recognizable buildings in this volcanically active area.

Still, the Soviets and scientists in Eastern European countries have often taken Atlantis more seriously than the Americans have. Zdenek Kukal, a skeptical Czech geologist, considered the possibility that the current islands of the mid-Atlantic ridge are the remains of Atlantis. All the islands on the ridge are extremely volcanic and unstable. The Azores, located west of Spain, are one of the most likely locations for Atlantis. All lie on an extensive submarine plateau that has a depth of a little more than a mile and an area of about 50,000 square miles. The Azores are an active site of seafloor spreading, and have substantial earthquake and volcanic activity. There are many flat-topped submarine peaks in the area. Of special interest is a major gravity anomaly, indicating an excess of mass under the Azores plateau. Also intriguing is the presence of numerous stone pebbles of non-local origin: granite, sandstone, limestone, and others, with no good explanation of how they got there.

The entire plateau is older than the Miocene (a geological period that ended roughly 7 million years ago), and must have started forming when the Atlantic Ocean began expanding in the Cretaceous period, which ended roughly 65 million years ago. Substantial parts of the plateau were once above water, and there has been a great deal of uplift and downfaulting in the past. Kukal, however, like most other geologists, does not accept the idea of recent catastrophes. He agrees that most of the Atlantic islands, including the larger ones, were formed in relatively short and sporadic periods of volcanic activity separated by much longer periods of quiescence. But he feels it is unlikely that the Azores plateau could have been above water to any great degree in 10,000 B.C.

One of the most intriguing pieces of evidence was published by R. W. Kolbe, a Swedish geologist, in 1957. Kolbe studied cores drilled at a depth of about two miles in the mid-Atlantic ridge between the Caribbean and North Africa, in what might have been the southern portion of Atlantis. He reported in *Science* finds of exclusively freshwater plants (diatoms) in portions of the cores. He concluded, in part, that this portion of the mid-Atlantic ridge was once above sea level, and that the diatoms had originated in a fresh water lake. Kolbe discusses Atlantis as a serious proposition. He cites another geologist, René Malaise, who felt that parts of the mid-Atlantic ridge must have existed as large islands up to the end of the last ice age or later, and were submerged in early historical times.

Kolbe's finds and similar discoveries led skeptics to try to explain them away. The two main explanations were windblown dust, and undersea "turbidity currents" that carried material from continental rivers. Many geologists favor these alternative explanations. For example, J. K. Rigby and L. H. Burckle, in a 1958 *Science* article, preferred the turbidity current explanation; others have presented evidence that windblown sand might explain deep-sea sand far from land. Kolbe answered these criticisms by pointing out that either mechanism would likely lead to mixtures of freshwater and oceanic diatoms, whereas he found a layer of pure freshwater diatoms. Still, the debate continues—often with much heat, but on a scientific, not an occult level.

The most extensive serious study of the possibility of Atlantis was published by Soviet scientist N. Zhirov in 1970. Zhirov discusses the great complexity of the geology of the mid-Atlantic ridge, citing over 800 references, and faulting American geologists for being unaware of foreign publications, especially Soviet ones! It is Zhirov's contention that the freshwater diatoms, deep-sea pebbles and sand, and eroded terraces on the mid-Atlantic ridge are true anomalies, suggesting that large parts of the ridge were once above water. Whether Zhirov is right awaits further evidence, but he is certainly more thorough than his critics.

So, the possibility certainly exists that major parts of the mid-Atlantic ridge could have been above water in the time frame given by Cayce, but most geologists would say that there is no conclusive evidence at this time. The mid-Atlantic ridge is active in terms of volcanoes and earthquakes, but it would have required a greater recent catastrophe than is currently accepted to submerge major parts of it near 10,000 B.C.

What of the deep Atlantic Ocean basin, away from the ridge? Could it have been above water? ". . . that portion now near what would be termed the Sargasso Sea first went into the depths . . ." (no. 364–4, February 16, 1932).

Cayce's statement about the Sargasso Sea, in the middle of the ocean basin, is more problematic than the speculation about the mid-Atlantic ridge. The Sargasso Sea is a large area in the Atlantic where the currents cause the accumulation of great amounts of floating seaweed. The floating Sargasso weed inspired fear of shoals in the days of Columbus. But by Cayce's time, depth soundings had shown the Sargasso Sea to be one of the deepest areas of the Atlantic Ocean, and that the Sargasso weed is not attached to the bottom. The bottom lies at over three miles below sea level, and is part of the Atlantic deep ocean basin. It is so flat that these areas are called abyssal plains.

In recent years, we have learned much more about the ocean bottom through the efforts of the Deep Sea Drilling Project. This project has drilled cores through the sediments in the sea bottom to sample fossil plankton (microscopic plants and animals) in order to determine the history of the sediments. Cores drilled by the Deep Sea Drilling Project reveal thick layers of deep ocean sediments. Thus, although Cayce's statement that the Sargasso Sea was the first area of Atlantis to go into the depths may be true, geologists agree that it happened millions of years ago, not thousands. It does not fit in with the time scale of the rest of the Cayce material on Atlantis.

Although the general picture of thick deep-sea sediments weakens the case for the recent surfacing of the Atlantic Ocean basin, most cores through the sediments reveal occasional large gaps, sometimes spanning millions of years. These could be explained in three ways. First, the ancient conditions of the ocean might have prevented sediments from being laid down for a period of time. Alternatively, the sediment layers could have been eroded away by something like the turbidity currents mentioned previously. Finally, the entire area could briefly have been above water, where no oceanic sediments would have been deposited. Geologists do not favor this idea, because it requires a catastrophe, and no areas of the deep ocean bottom are currently above water. Nevertheless, there are still some anomalies that are difficult to explain.

Two locations studied in the ocean basin away from the mid-Atlantic ridge are of special relevance to the Cayce Atlantis. One is the area of the Bermuda rise, an area rising from the deep-sea bottom in the western North Atlantic, which is another likely candidate for the sunken Atlantis. In general, the results from the deep-sea cores confirmed the concept that this area has been deep ocean for over 80 million years. However, a February 1977 article in *Science News* announced that buried in the sediments was a group of rounded, highly polished pebbles that bear a strong resemblance to the wave-worn pebbles found on beaches. No conclusions could be drawn at that time; but it may mean that the site, one of the deepest parts of the Atlantic, was once nearly at sea level.

The other area of interest is the Blake plateau, a shallow, submerged area north of the Bahamas that was reported on in *Geotimes* in February 1976. The cores of the Blake plateau show that it was indeed formed above water as a coral reef, but in the Cretaceous period, over 65 million years ago. Unfortunately for the Atlantis hypothesis, this is probably the last time the Blake plateau was above water. Millions of years of ocean sediments overlay it; but the geology is complex, and some geological periods of sediments are completely missing. Although this could be evidence that the area was above water at the time, geologists prefer other explanations, such as erosion of sediments by turbidity currents or lack of deposition due to unfavorable water conditions. Geologists need clear evidence of land deposits, such as freshwater fossils, to be convinced that this area may have been above water.

Perhaps Atlantis lay nearer to the continents, or even included the continental shelf. It is well known that large areas of the continental shelf were submerged by the rising sea level when the glaciers melted. One area that all geologists would agree was above water, and which was submerged at the time given by Cayce, was also the only area given by Cayce as a specific location for the ruins of Atlantis: the Bahama bank. The Bahama bank is a plateau that begins about 45 miles east of the coast of Florida, and covers an area as large as Florida. The island nearest Florida is known as Bimini: "Yes, we have the land known as Bimini, in the Atlantic Ocean . . . this is the highest portion left above the waves of a once great continent, upon which the civilization as now exists in the world's history found much of that as would be used as means for attaining that civilization" (no. 996–1, August 14, 1926).

The Bahama bank as a location for Atlantis is unique to Cayce. Neither the occultists nor the scholarly Atlantologists had ever considered it. Yet it was indisputably above water at the time given by Cayce, and was submerged by the melting of the glaciers around 10,000 B.C.

Is it reasonable to look for the ruins of Atlantis in the Bahamas? That it was above water in 10,000 B.C. is well proved by such studies as that of J. D. Milliman and K. O. Emery, published in *Science* in 1968. They were able to determine ancient sea levels going back 35,000 years. Human occupation at this time has become increasingly likely in the light of recent evidence of ancient occupation of Florida and the Caribbean islands. An article in *Science* in 1979 describes how a team led by Carl Clausen, a Florida archaeologist, found evidence of human occupation dating to at least 12,000 years ago submerged in sinkholes in Florida. Shell middens (piles of accumulated waste) and other remains have been found dating back several thousand years in Cuba and Hispaniola, the two closest islands to the Bahamas, according to archaeologists José Cruxent and Irving Rouse in an article in *Scientific American* in November 1969. Mammoth teeth have been found in ancient coastal areas submerged by rising water from the melting of the glaciers, according to an article published in *Science* in 1967 by a group of geologists including F. C. Whitmore and K. O. Emery. Emery's group has also searched for human artifacts on the U.S. continental shelf. It is not unreasonable to speculate that the Bahama bank was occupied when it was above water, although no evidence of such occupation has yet been accepted by mainstream archaeologists.

Chapter six will discuss the current search for Atlantis near Bimini.

What of the time factor? Could Atlantis have been submerged in a relatively sudden flood, causing the destruction of a civilization? The readings say, "In those latter periods, ten thousand seven hundred [10,700] years before the Prince of Peace came . . . the *wasting* away in the mountains, then into the valleys, then into the sea itself, and the fast disintegration of the lands . . ." (no. 364–3, February 16, 1932).

One of the major forces that shaped the world during the time of Cayce's Atlantis were the glaciers, vast sheets of ice which advanced southward, covering everything in their path. Tremendous amounts of water were locked up in this ice, lowering sea level perhaps hundreds of feet from where it is today. This alone would have placed areas such as Bimini above water. The glaciers advanced and receded many times over thousands of years, until the final retreat near 10,000 B.C., very close to the time given by both Cayce and Plato for the final Atlantean destruction. Reading no. 364–3, quoted above, is an excellent description of the melting of the glaciers. In North America, the meltwater carved out the Chesapeake Bay, and piled sediments on the eastern shore. It created Long Island, New York, from the thousands of tons of rock and debris it had pushed ahead. It flooded huge areas of the continental shelf.

How fast did it happen? In a single day as claimed by Plato; over hundreds of years, as implied by Cayce; or over thousands of years, as geologists thought in Cayce's time? In 1979, geologist Hermann Flohn of the University of Bonn in West Germany reviewed some evidence that could be used to support the Cayce scenario. Flohn was looking at how fast the glaciers formed. In an article in *Quaternary Research* in 1979, he reported that, based on cores drilled through the ice at Camp Century, Greenland, there was a virtually instantaneous change (geologically speaking, within about a hundred years) from a climate warmer than the present into full glacial severity. Flohn discussed what he terms "convincing evidence" for a close relation between glaciation, major volcanic eruptions, and clusters of severe earthquakes. He noted that within a "human" time scale of a hundred years or less, our climate can change *much* more rapidly than hitherto assumed.

Can the same be said for the *melting* of the glaciers? Strong evidence for the suddenness of a flood of meltwater was presented in *Science* in 1975 by Cesare Emiliani, a noted marine geologist at the University of Miami. The Emiliani article is significant, because it specifically mentions Plato's story and the date he gave, 9600 B.C., which is fairly close to the spread of Cayce's dates. Emiliani drilled cores into the bottom of the Gulf of Mexico. Using data received from oxygen isotope tests to measure ancient temperatures, radiocarbon for dating, and fossil evidence, he identified an episode of rapid glacial ice melting and sea level rise that could well be termed a "flood."

THE SHIFTING OF THE POLES

What other evidence is there that the great destructions spoken of by Cayce could have taken place? The concept of pole shifts, also linked with climatic change and extinctions, is key to the concept of catastrophic geological changes in the Cayce readings. The evidence for pole shifts linked with volcanoes, earthquakes, extinctions of animals, and climatic changes is some of the strongest support for the Cayce story.

The readings mention pole shifts in connection both with earth changes in the ancient past and earth changes in our future:

> You see, with the changes—when there came the uprisings in the Atlantean land, and the sojourning southward—with the turning of the axis . . . (no. 364–13, A-8, November 17, 1932)
> . . . the changes wrought in the upheavals and the shifting of the poles . . . (no. 378–16, October 29, 1933)
> . . . There will be upheavals in the Arctic in the Antarctic that will make for the eruption of volcanoes in the Torrid areas, and there will be the shifting then of the poles—so that where there has been those of a frigid or the semi-tropical will become the more tropical, and the moss and fern will grow. (no. 3976–15, January 19, 1934)

What is a pole shift? There are two types of poles on the earth: the geographic poles and the magnetic poles. The geographic poles are the ends of the axis on which the earth rotates, called "true" north and south. The other poles are the ones to which a magnetic compass needle points, called "magnetic" north and south. Right now the magnetic north pole is somewhere in Canada, several hundred miles from the geographic pole, and it moves a little every year. For most places in the world, the difference is not too serious. In Virginia Beach, for example, the difference is only about three degrees. The cause for the earth's magnetic field and poles is not known, but it appears to be linked with the rotation of the earth.

There is evidence that either or both of the pole types have shifted in the past, and virtually all of it has accumulated after the Cayce readings were given. In Cayce's time, the only evidence of possible pole shifts was that tropical fossils are often found in temperate areas. This could have been evidence for a pole shift, but it could also have simply been evidence for a worldwide warming trend.

Magnetic Pole Shifts, Climatic Change, and Extinctions

In the 1960s, when much of the work confirming continental drift was done, measurement of magnetic pole reversals was somewhat crude. Pole reversals were then thought to occur about every million years, with the most recent around 700,000 years ago. In the 1970s, however, scientists made discoveries that tallied exactly with the Cayce dates for the destructions of Atlantis. The readings state, ". . . the entity was in Atlantis when there was the second period of disturbance—which would be some twenty-two thousand, five hundred (22,500) [years] before the periods of activity covered by the Exodus; or it was some twenty-eight thousand (28,000) [years] before Christ, see?" (no. 470–22, July 5, 1938).

In a 1972 article in *Nature*, two Australian geologists, Michael Barbetti and Michael McElhinney, announced the discovery of a reversal of the magnetic poles, dated to 30,000 years ago (28,000 B.C.)—exactly the date given by Cayce for a destruction of Atlantis. The find was preserved in the fireplaces of ancient humans in Australia. Barbetti and McElhinney studied lumps of clay, whose magnetic field orientations had been preserved when they were baked in the fire. Radiocarbon dating of the charcoal in the fireplace gave the age. When they compared their result with those of other studies, they concluded that the pole reversal had lasted less than 4,000 years, far too brief a time to show up in measurements of deep-sea magnetism.

Cayce talked about a shifting of the poles that was linked with ice and the destruction of large animals: "The entity then was among those who were of that group who gathered to rid the earth of the enormous animals which overran the earth, but ice, the entity found, nature, God, changed the poles and the animals were destroyed, though man attempted it in the activity of the meetings" (no. 5249–1, June 12, 1944).

Two of the Cayce dates fit this scenario, those for the first and last destructions. The first, the one referred to in the quote, was 50,772 B.C., the time of the world meeting. No pole reversal has yet been discovered for this date, but the correspondence to a major extinction of large animals is very good. Paul Martin, of the University of Arizona, dates a catastrophic extinction of large animals in Africa at the end of the Acheulean period of archaeological technology, at about fifty thousand years ago. In an article in *Nature* in 1966, Martin explained his feeling that the extinctions are clearly related to the spread of human beings and their cultural development. The Acheulean culture of this time used crude stone tools, including large hand-axes and cleavers, which were of intercontinental distribution. The Acheuleans were replaced around the date Cayce gives for the first destruction by much more specialized Middle Stone Age cultures.

An even more exciting confirmation of the readings, combining all the elements mentioned by Cayce, came from a pole reversal known as the Gothenburg magnetic "flip" because of its short duration, this time near the date given by Cayce for the final destruction of Atlantis about 10,000 B.C. This was the most frequently mentioned date in the readings; many readings gave specific dates from 10,000 B.C. to 10,700 B.C.

The Swedish geologists Nils-Axel Morner and Johan Lanser, reporting in *Nature* in 1974, first recognized the Gothenburg flip from measurements of a core taken in the Botanical Gardens at Gothenburg, Sweden. Since then, the flip has been confirmed by other researchers from around the world. It was short, not more than two thousand years, and lasted until about 12,400 to 12,350 years ago (about 10,400 to 10,350 B.C.), exactly in the middle of the Cayce range.

In 1977, Rhodes Fairbridge, a geologist from Columbia University in New York, published a paper in *Nature* on the Gothenburg flip that closely paralleled the Cayce scenario. Fairbridge looked at the relation of the pole shift to global climates. During much of the time of Cayce's Atlantis, when glaciers covered large parts of North America and Europe, large animals or "megafauna" roamed the world: mammoths, giant ground sloths, saber-toothed tigers. Fairbridge noted that, at the time of the reversal, although the glaciers were in the process of melting, for a short time the ice came again. There was a brief, but intense cooling. He noted specifically that major changes in human evolution are linked with pole reversals of this type. As we will see in the next chapter, Paul Martin has even more to say about unusual extinctions at the time of the final destruction of Atlantis.

A study published in *Nature* in 1977 by J. P. Kennett and N. D. Watkins, of the Graduate School of Oceanography at the University of Rhode Island, can also be used to support the Cayce concepts. This study links much earlier polar reversals not only with extinctions, but also with periods of high earthquake and volcanic activity. The extinctions addressed in their study were of microscopic marine plankton. The evidence in support of pole reversals associated with catastrophes of volcanic activity, climatic change, and extinctions is strong. It doesn't prove Cayce was right about Atlantis, but he was certainly ahead of his time with his concepts of geology.

One other date mentioned in the readings also correlates with climatic change, although the date was not specific enough for a precise match. Reading no. 364–11 mentions a date for a destruction that is 7,500 years before the final destruction (or about 18,000 B.C., depending on exactly which date is taken for the final destruction). This is fairly close to the time when the glaciers began their final retreat; it is linked with widespread climatic changes, although not with known pole shifts.

Geographic Pole Shifts

Most of this evidence has addressed magnetic pole shifts. What about about geographic pole shifts? Although he is not always specific, Cayce seems to be referring to a shift of the rotational axis of the earth. The magnetic poles seem to be produced by the spinning of the earth, but the evidence for actual shifts of the spin axis has been ambiguous.

Author John White, in *Pole Shift*, discusses the various theories of geographic pole shifts. Back in Cayce's time, the scientific consensus (based on analyses by physicist James Clerk Maxwell and Sir George Darwin, son of Charles Darwin) was that no conceivable force originating within the earth could make it shift on its axis. More recently, the fossil evidence has been interpreted in terms of continental drift—the poles are stationary, but the continents drift about and produce apparent pole shifts. It is clear that continental drift has occurred; but does this rule out pole shifts?

In 1955, Thomas Gold reexamined the question in an article in the journal *Nature*. He postulated that the earth's wobble on its axis could cause a plastic flow of the interior of the earth that would read-just the bulge at the equator. Thus large polar wandering could be expected to occur over periods of geological time, and the earth may have rolled over several times during its history. The time frame for Gold's pole reversal was on the order of 10,000 to 1 million years.

More recently, in 1978, Edward Weyer revived Gold's idea in a *Nature* article. He warned that an ice age could be the trigger mechanism for some degree of pole slippage, thus linking geographic pole shifts with climatic change. Weyer's research showed that there have been rhythmic oscillations of the poles on a 5,600-year cycle, synchronized with the periods of the glaciers from 14,700 to 28,000 years ago, right in the heyday of Cayce's Atlantis.

The most recent serious consideration of a *rapid* geographic pole reversal was published in the prestigious *Journal of Physics* in 1978. Peter Warlow, a British physicist and mathematician, proposed that it is not the magnetic field that reverses itself, but the earth turning upside down within it. He calculated that a disturbance, from a passing asteroid, for example, could exert enough gravitational pull to make the earth topple over. Such an event could take place in as little time as a day! Warlow's paper is speculative, but backed with detailed analyses.

These ideas about geographic pole shifts are still minority viewpoints among geologists. Most feel that little polar wandering has occurred, and that movement of continental plates is enough to explain the distribution of tropical and temperate fossils. Still, the concept is very much alive, and may indeed be proved in the future. Meanwhile, the evidence for magnetic pole shifts and their link with earthquakes, volcanoes, climatic change, and extinctions is clear. Cayce's statements, when applied to magnetic pole shifts, are entirely consistent with modern scientific thought, both in theoretical concept and specific dates.

On the whole, the revolution in geology has tended to support the Cayce concepts, though with great reservation about the existence of Atlantis itself. It allows for parts of the Atlantic Ocean (not necessarily "continent") to have been above water. Geologists have independently tied together the mechanisms for change proposed in the Cayce readings: pole reversals, earthquakes, volcanoes, and glacial melting. But what of the evidence for the Atlanteans themselves: their buildings, their culture, their bones? For this, we must turn to archaeology.

4
THE TESTIMONY OF ARCHAEOLOGY

THE READINGS' CLAIMS for the existence of Atlantis were controversial, but they fit into a general context of "catastrophic geology," which in some aspects is becoming more accepted by mainstream geologists. But the story of human origins and the migrations from Atlantis directly contradicted the opinion of the archaeology establishment of Cayce's time. It sounded to them like the Donnelly idea revisited—the simplistic statement that fleeting Atlanteans were responsible for the Egyptian, Maya, and Inca civilizations. Even in Cayce's time, archaeologists could see that Donnelly's parallels had many errors, and that the dates for his offshoots from Atlantis missed by thousands of years.

But the Cayce story differs from Donnelly in some very important ways. While archaeological discoveries have tended to make many of Donnelly's speculations less likely, they often have tended to make the Cayce version *more* likely. The Cayce readings speak of much more than the migrations at the final destruction of Atlantis. They begin with the origin of humankind, trace its repeated rise and fall through three destructions of Atlantis, and tell of migrants to various areas of the world. This chapter will look at what archaeology has to say in comparison to Cayce's story of origins and migrations.

THE ORIGIN OF HUMANKIND

Like the Theosophists, Cayce was not simply trying to explain our physical origin, but our spiritual origins as well. Unlike the Theosophists, however, Cayce presented a relatively clear, simplified picture of human origin and evolution. There were no "Polareans" or "Hyperboreans"; no gigantic Lemurians with jelly-like bodies, no foreheads, and eyes on the sides of their heads. Cayce did speak of the descent of the human spirit into physical bodies, and his spiritual concepts are difficult to interpret in the light of science. But the Cayce physical descriptions of ancient people, though controversial, were within the realm of the serious scientific speculation of his day. Much of what he said seems even more likely to be true today, though there are still some anomalies science would find hard to accept.

When the earth brought forth the seed in her season, and man came in the earth plane as the lord of that in that sphere, man appeared in five places then at once—the five senses, the five reasons, the five spheres, the five developments, the five nations. (no. 5748–1, May 28, 1925)

The period in the world's existence from the present time being ten and one-half million (10,500,000) years. . . . (no. 5748–2, May 28, 1925)

. . . in the ruins as are found that have arisen, in the mounds and caves in the northwestern portion of New Mexico, may be seen some of the drawings the entity then made. Some ten million years ago. (no. 2665–2, July 17, 1925)

These [Atlanteans] took on many sizes as to stature, from that as may be called midgets to the giants—for there were giants in the earth in those days. (no. 364–11, April 29, 1932)

The theories of human origins, in Cayce's time as well as today, have led to some of the greatest controversies in the history of science—we can't begin to cover them in these few pages. Our goal here is to examine what light, if any, science can shed on the following questions arising from the Cayce readings:

• Did human beings first appear around 10 million years ago?

- Is there any evidence of human culture in the distant past?
- What is the origin of race? Were there five root races, and any evidence for ''midgets'' or ''giants''?
- Where did human beings first appear, and in what time frame did they disperse throughout the world?

What does science consider evidence of early human beings? Of our spiritual origin, there is little science can say. Much of the material in *The Coming of Man*, discussed in chapter two, is in the realm of theology. Rudolf Steiner, whose theories were discussed in chapter one, was probably right when he said that clairvoyant perception was the most useful method for gathering this kind of information. Some statements in the readings about early human beings, however, can be verified or refuted using the scientific method. Science can only deal with the physical remains: our artifacts and our bones. At first thought, it might seem simple—evidence consists of a fossil skeleton, dated to a specific time in the past.

Unfortunately, it's not so easy. Fossil evidence is extremely rare, and complete skeletons are unheard of. Sometimes species may be identified from a single tooth. Most theories of human evolution are based on fragments of skulls and jaws. Other evidence includes stone tools and ashes from fires. The problem is that these artifacts are often found without bones, so the species can only be inferred. Even with modern dating methods, geological deposits are often so complex that accurate dating is difficult. Nevertheless, great advances have been made, and likely human ancestors have now been found dating back at least 3 million years and possibly even longer.

Concepts of Origins in Cayce's Time

What was the thinking on human origin and evolution in Cayce's time? Cayce lived in the midst of a heated debate on this subject. The famous Scopes ''monkey trial'' occurred in 1925, pitting Darwinian evolution against biblical creationism. This trial of a high school teacher for teaching evolution ignited national and international interest, and paved the way for the widespread acceptance of evolutionary thought. However, it did little to clear up the question of human ancestry. The fossil record in Cayce's time was so meager that almost any theory could be derived from it.

The first fossils of an ancient human relative, known as Neanderthal man, were discovered in 1848 on the island of Gibraltar. Another fossil, for which the type is named, was discovered in Germany's Neander valley in 1856. Neanderthal man became the prototype "cave man," and in Cayce's time the accepted consensus among evolutionists was that Neanderthal man was an intermediate form between apes and men. By the 1930s, even more primitive ancient bones were found, including Java man and Peking man. All that could be said with certainty at this time was that primitive forms of human beings existed, and they were of indeterminate age. The "missing link" between apes and human beings was still a matter of conjecture, as absolute dating techniques had not yet been invented. The best candidate for the missing link in Cayce's time was Piltdown man, discovered in 1912, and now known to be a clever forgery formed from a combination of a human skull with an ape's jaw. Kenneth Oakley in the *American Scientist* used modern dating methods in 1953 to show that the Piltdown skull was only a few hundred years old.

Cayce's first reading mentioning the 10-million-year-old date was given in 1925. This was the same year the first evidence for truly ancient human relatives was discovered, though it was not recognized at the time. The Taung skull, now known to be around 3 million years old, was discovered by anthropologist Raymond Dart in 1925; at the time, it was met with a mixture of scorn and indifference from the archaeological community. Roger Lewin, in a 1985 *Science* article, notes that Dart, basing his opinion on the geological context, felt the skull was very ancient. But in 1925, the age of the earth itself was considered to be just 65 million years, with mammals squeezed into the last 3 million years. The anthropologists of the time felt that a fossil this old simply couldn't be a human ancestor—the human race was at the most a few thousand years old.

Thus the Cayce readings did not fit comfortably into contemporary scientific opinion. They supported the concept of great antiquity in human lineage—a position now known to be consistent with the fossil evidence of the day, but not with its interpretation at that time. On the other hand, although Cayce said that the human race was far more ancient than science would accept, he contradicted the popular version of evolution when he stated, ". . . Man *did not* descend from the monkey, but man has evolved, resuscitation, you see, from time to time . . ." (no. 3744–4, A-46, February 14, 1924).

He also ran afoul of the creationists, stating, "Let it be remembered, or not confused, that the *earth* was peopled by *animals* before peopled by man!" (no. 364–6, February 17, 1932); and, in reference to our ancestors, "See, most of the people had tails then!" (no. 5748–6, July 1, 1932).

The Cayce position was unique, and could expect little support from either the science or religion of its time. Have we learned anything since then that might shed light on whether Cayce was right or wrong?

Current Concepts of Human Origins

Scientifically, the theory of evolution has won the day; but the controversy over human origins has not abated at all since Cayce's time. If anything, it has intensified. Modern "monkey trials," pitting creationists against evolutionists, are still going on. Even among evolutionists, there is still considerable disagreement over what is and what is not evidence for human ancestry.

A good, popular presentation, although somewhat controversial in its interpretations of the fossil evidence, is *Lucy: The Beginnings of Humankind*, by Donald Johanson and Maitland Edey. Johanson discovered bones over 3 million years old that may well belong to a direct human ancestor. Johanson's is by no means the last word. Books such as *The Bone Peddlers*, by William Fix, highlight the gaps in our understanding by pointing out the varied interpretations that can be applied to the sparse fossil remains. Overall, however, many of Cayce's statements seem substantially more likely now than they did back in the 1930s, especially in regard to the antiquity of human ancestors, and the simultaneous presence of several species of various sizes. Although people and monkeys had a common biological ancestor in the distant past, that ancestor appears to have existed prior to Cayce's 10-million-year date for the descent of the spirit into the physical plane. Since then, the evolutionary picture has become confusing and complex.

A multitude of fossils have been discovered since Cayce's time, but they have complicated rather than simplified the story. Ever since the invention of modern dating techniques, the ages for ancient human relatives have been pushed back into the more and more distant past. The primary controversy today is over which fossil species are actually human ancestors, and which are offshoots in other directions. Even Neanderthal man is no longer thought to be in the direct line of human descent.

But one Cayce point is clearly confirmed: many forms of human or humanoid creatures lived thousands and even millions of years ago, both giants and dwarfs. Species named *Ramapithecus, Gigantopithecus*, and *Australopithecus* all may have been our ancient relatives.

Ramapithecus, an ancient primate (the classification that includes monkeys, apes, and humans) is one possible candidate for a human ancestor. *Ramapithecus* was small, only a few feet high. In 1964, as cited in William Fix's book, paleontologist Elwyn Simons wrote, "*Ramapithecus punjabicus* is almost certainly man's forerunner of 15 million years ago. This determination increases tenfold the approximate time period during which human origins can now be traced with some confidence." This view was echoed by many writers throughout the 1970s, although recent opinion has assigned *Ramapithecus* to a side branch in evolution.

The Cayce biblical quote, "There were giants in the earth in those days" (Genesis 6:4), was confirmed with the discovery of the huge bones of *Gigantopithecus* in 1946, dated back to nearly 10 million years ago. *Gigantopithecus* stood more than 8 feet tall and weighed 400 to 500 pounds. In the 1940s, *Gigantopithecus* was thought to be a good candidate for a missing link; but, like *Ramapithecus*, it is now thought to be an evolutionary side branch.

The fossils of *Gigantopithecus* and *Ramapithecus*, if not human ancestors, were contemporary with our true ancestor. These primates were indeed giants and dwarfs, and some lived earlier than 10 million years ago, when Cayce said human beings first appeared. These were not anatomically modern people; our ancestors likely did have "tails then!" Current scientific opinion is that the best candidate for a direct ancestor of man is a primate named *Australopithecus*.

Australopithecus dates back nearly 4 million years. Donald Johanson gave the name "Lucy" to a 40 percent-complete *Australopithecus* skeleton he discovered in Africa in 1974. Lucy is remarkable in that never before had so much of such an old hominid skeleton been recovered. Lucy's leg bones indicate that she walked erect, just as we do. Exactly how closely Lucy is related to modern humans is still very much in debate; but the discovery adds even more weight to the concept of the great antiquity of the line leading to modern human beings.

Although these creatures walked upright, and may have been our ancestors, we are also defined by culture. The Cayce readings speak of high cultural achievements in the distant past. What evidence do we have of such a culture?

Louis Leakey, one of the great discoverers of early human fossils, has found the earliest, unequivocally dated stone tools in East Africa produced by *Australopithecus* or early species of *Homo* (our own genus), dating to about 2.61 million years ago. In 1986, as reported by Bruce Bower in *Science News*, nearly 300 stone tools apparently produced by *Homo habilis*, a very close relative of *Homo sapiens*, have been dated to 2.5 million years ago. In addition to the evidence from tools, anatomist Dean Falk of the University of Puerto Rico reported in *Science* in 1983 that he had found human-like brain patterns in fossil skulls dated approximately 2 million years old from East Africa, and 3 million years old from South Africa.

Considering the antiquity of these finds, even stone tools are impressive evidence that whatever they may have looked like, these creatures were certainly more than the "monkeys" of popular evolution in Cayce's time. They show that our link with the other primates is millions of years older than was believed in the 1920s. But Cayce spoke of more than stone tools. He spoke of what today we would call "high technology," apparently describing lasers, atomic energy, and flying machines. His readings describing the high technological achievements of ancient people are among his most controversial. No evidence has yet been found of the sorts of technology he spoke of, especially millions, or even thousands, of years ago. Clearly, one problem with finding such evidence is that stone preserves well, while metals, wood, paper, and other such materials decay. As we will see in the next chapter, the Cayce readings specify some locations where records of this high technology may be found. Still, scientists today would view Cayce's technology descriptions with skepticism, to say the least.

Nevertheless, there is at least some evidence that ancient people were surprisingly sophisticated culturally. Alexander Marshack, in the January 1975 issue of *National Geographic*, discusses a bone artifact from an Ice Age people that is a record of astronomical observations. The carvings on a fragment of reindeer bone, which are at least 30,000 years old, show with startling precision a chronicle of the phases of the moon, a level of understanding far greater than one would expect of "primitive" people. Marshack also discusses how, in 1969, a French geologist and archaeologist named François Bordes published a paper on the discovery of an unusually engraved ox rib over 250,000 years old from a cave in France. The symbolism of the carvings is unknown; but Marshack demonstrated that they were put there deliberately, showing a sequential structure and image. Marshack feels that such images are proof of intelligence, abstraction, and even a use of language.

There is more evidence of human culture. It seems that even Neanderthal man had respect for the dead, and was concerned with the spiritual journey. In an article in *Science* in 1975, archaeologist R. S. Solecki comments that the discovery of pollen clusters of different kinds of flowers in the graves of one of the Neanderthals at Shanidar Cave, Iraq, dating to 60,000 B.C., was presumably part of a funeral ritual. It suggests that, although the body was archaic, the spirit was modern.

Meanwhile, as with human antiquity, the antiquity of technology is continually being pushed back. In 1975 in *Science*, Fred Wendorf of Southern Methodist University dated sophisticated stone tools in central Ethiopia, which indicate that the Middle Stone Age of East Africa began prior to 180,000 years ago. As recently as 1970, the oldest date was thought to have been around 40,000 years ago. This suggests that the technological developments that characterize the Middle Stone Age have a far greater antiquity than previously estimated.

We have far less evidence of truly advanced technology. Only artifacts much more recent than the dates given in the readings have ever been found. The ancient Greeks may have had batteries and calculating machines, according to some reports; but the fact that it has been so difficult to identify even the technology of the Greeks—a well-documented culture—only speaks to the problem of Atlantis by showing how hard it would be to confirm the presence of prehistoric technology. The very ancient high technology of which the readings spoke is still nowhere to be found; but the finds of archaeology continue to show that the human mind, if not human technology, was advanced beyond the comprehension of archaeologists in Cayce's day.

THE ORIGIN OF RACES AND THE DISPERSAL OF HUMANKIND

What of Cayce's statements on the origin of races? Cayce spoke of five root races:

[Q-5.] Did the appearance of what became the five races occur simultaneously? [A-5.] Occurred at once. (no. 364–13, November 17, 1932)

[Q-7.] Are the following the correct places? Atlantean the red (race)?

[A-7.] Atlantean and American, the red race.

[Q-8.] Upper Africa for the black?

[A-8.] Or what would be known now as the more western portion of upper Egypt for the black. You see, with the changes—when there came the uprisings in the Atlantean land, and the sojourning southward—with the turning of the axis, the white and yellow races came more into that portion of Egypt, India, Persia, and Arabia. (no. 364–13, November 17, 1932)

Asia was considered to be the cradle of humanity back in 1932, following the discovery of Java man and Peking man.

The many discoveries in Africa were yet to come, and no ancient remains of any kind had been found in America. Fossil bones and stone tools could tell us little about human racial types, and the theories of the origin of races in the past have had strong racist overtones. That is, a white European anthropologist might say that Africans or Australian aborigines were more closely related to apes than white Europeans.

Cayce confounded the racists—he said that the five races had appeared simultaneously. This contrasted with the occult doctrine, with its confusing array of seven Root Races, each with seven subraces. It also provided no support for the theories of white racial superiority. The occultists spoke of the Aryans, our current white race, as descended from the Atlanteans. Cayce's Atlanteans, purported to be the most sophisticated culture in the world, were identified as the red race, closest to the Native Americans, who were then considered primitives.

Cayce clearly identified the white race as originating in the Caucasus region of Asia, in agreement with modern anthropological thought. When asked to clarify the location, he said, "The white—rather in the Carpathians than India. . . . Southern part of Europe and Russia, and Persia and that land. Caucasian mountains" (no. 364–13, November 17, 1932).

What does science say today about the origin of races? Were there five, and could they have originated simultaneously in different parts of the world?

The first scientific study of race closely paralleling the Cayce story was a controversial book called *The Origin of Races*, published in 1962. The author was a noted anthropologist, Carleton Coon of the University of Pennsylvania. Prior to Coon, races were thought to be a relatively recent phenomenon. Presumably, they all differentiated from each other after human beings had evolved to fully modern form, perhaps 30,000 years ago. Coon's thesis, like Cayce's, was that there were five basic races, and that they had evolved in parallel over hundreds of thousands of years. Coon felt that a single human species existed 500,000 years ago, *Homo erectus*, and that he could trace modern racial characteristics back to the skeletal features of *Homo erectus* in different areas of the world. If true, this would closely correspond to the Cayce version of the five races appearing in remote antiquity. Coon even speculated that the *Homo* lineage might go back 8 million years, also in close agreement with Cayce. Since some of Coon's statements implied that the black races were more primitive, Coon's book was quite controversial at the time. Now his theory represents only one perspective in a variety of explanations for the appearance of modern people.

Most anthropologists today believe that the concept of race itself is an oversimplification of the genetic diversity of the human species. The makeup of populations has shifted so frequently during the course of migrations that sharp demarcations are few, and differences in visible physical features are not always sure guides to differences in ancestry. According to anthropologist Clyde Kluckhohn, the number of races distinguished by competent students ranges from two to two hundred. Considering the extent of the ancient migrations described in the Cayce readings, it would be difficult to establish the validity of the symbolic number of "five" root races.

The latest theories on human origins were the subject of a conference in 1987 at Cambridge University in England, reported in *Science* by Roger Lewin. The picture is complicated: theories based on analyses of genes and theories based on dating of bones compete. The question is whether modern people evolved in one location and migrated to the rest of the world, or evolved independently in several locations. The Cayce readings say five locations, but imply that migrations from Atlantis beginning around 50,000 years ago spread Atlanteans throughout the world. Thus in the present we might expect to see conflicting evidence.

A key point is the sudden replacement of Neanderthal man by Cro-Magnon man in Europe about 35,000 years ago. Cro-Magnon man was fully modern in appearance—both his height and skull capacity were above the average for modern Europeans. Anthropologists are still not sure where Cro-Magnon man came from. The date spread for the disappearance of the Neanderthals is quite wide; it happened 45,000 years ago in the Near East according to Lewin's article, and 32,000 years ago in Europe. The time frame is certainly consistent with Cayce's dates for migrations from Atlantis in

50,772 B.C. (no. 262–39, February 21, 1933) and 28,000 B.C. (no. 470–22, July 5, 1938).

One of the more intriguing parallels to the Cayce readings comes from recent work in genetics, reported in the British journal *New Scientist* on May 14, 1987. The readings said, "... the variations in Atlantis, as we find, extend over a period of some two hundred thousand [200,000] years ..." (no. 364–4, February 16, 1932). Biochemists Allan Wilson, Mark Stoneking, and Rebecca Cann of the University of California at Berkeley studied evolutionary relationships between racial groups. They looked at the genes in mitochondria, components of human cells inherited only from the mother. By comparing differences among races, and estimating rates of genetic change, they concluded that all living humans are descended from a common maternal ancestor, "Eve," who lived 200,000 years ago. That is, all living humans share these genes, and the divergence among races has occurred since this time. Could it have begun in Atlantis? Based on the relative diversity among the racial groups they have studied, these researchers feel that it was Africa, but of course they have no living Atlanteans for genetic comparisons.

Regarding the dispersion of humans throughout the world, another Cayce date is matched closely by the work of Christy Turner, an anthropologist from Arizona State University who studies tooth anatomy. Cayce referred to the first destruction of Atlantis in 50,772 B.C., a time at which there was a meeting of world leaders, indicating worldwide dispersion of humans (no. 262–39, February 21, 1933). By comparing the rates of tooth anatomy change in racial groups worldwide, Turner concluded that the date of dispersion of humanity was around fifty thousand years ago (*Science*). Such a measure is inexact, but is consistent with the Cayce readings. Turner's analysis, however, suggests that Native Americans have primarily Asian origins, supporting the opinion of most mainstream anthropologists, rather than the Cayce story. Turner's conservative approach to human antiquity suggests great skepticism regarding Atlantis (for example, see Turner's 1982 review of Jeffrey Goodman's book *American Genesis*, in *Archaeology*, Vol. 35, No. 1, p. 72). Still, Native American origins may be quite complex. We will return to this point in the next section, on migrations from Atlantis.

Scientists have no fossil finds from Atlantis itself, so it is not surprising that anthropologists do not consider Atlantis as a possible location for the original home of humankind. Still, the Cayce readings are amazingly in tune with modern concepts of human antiquity. As we will see in the next section, the indirect evidence of Atlantis from the migrations of ancient humans also provides interesting parallels with the Cayce readings. The work of Louis Leakey offers a possibility that human ancestors may have lived in North America as far back as 500,000 years ago.

One contention in the readings would still be rejected outright by modern biology: the Cayce concept of "things" that were part-human and part-animal, similar to the half-man, half-horse centaurs of Greek mythology. In the Cayce readings, things appeared early in human evolution as spiritual beings experimenting with life on the physical plane, and they existed right up until shortly after the final destruction of Atlantis around 10,000 B.C. The mythological concept of things is well known, not only from Greek mythology, but from drawings in Egyptian tombs of bird-headed gods, and from the body of the Sphinx itself. But is there any reason to believe these creatures actually lived?

The blunt answer is "no," both from an evolutionary and a creationist perspective. For once, both evolutionists and creationists would agree that their theories cannot accept the idea of animals made from the parts of two divergent lineages. For the evolutionists, humans and horses had a common ancestor; but they diverged in evolution, and people could not possibly have the gene for hooves. In the view of the creationists, humans and horses were created as two different "kinds" of animals, which could not mix. The problem for the Cayce material is that, even if it were true, it may be impossible to find convincing evidence because of limitations in the fossil record. Scientists reconstruct skeletons, often from a jumble of fossil bones, using evolutionary assumptions. Hooves found with a human skeleton would be assumed to be part of another animal. Carl Dunbar, in *Historical Geology*, makes the point well with a picture of mammoth bones reassembled as a unicorn (with a single tusk as the horn!) by an imaginative paleontologist in 1663. All reconstructions are driven by theory, and today's theories would consider "things" no more likely than unicorns.

There would have to be a major change in the basic concepts of biology before this Cayce concept could be taken seriously. However, recent progress in genetic engineering has elevated the idea of combining parts from different animals from the realm of fiction to the realm of science. No longer is there an insuperable barrier to creation of new forms of life. But modern genetic engineering is high technology, and no one has found any evidence of such a high technology in the ancient past. Was Cayce wrong? As we will see in the next section, the migrations from Atlantis took Atlanteans to many places, where the readings tell of buried records. Perhaps these records will have the answer.

THE MIGRATIONS FROM ATLANTIS

The major focus of most life readings mentioning Atlantis was not human origins, but rather the lives of individuals during the destructions of Atlantis and the migrations to safer lands. In chapter two we read about the lives of some of these people, with details of the story from the Cayce readings. As we have seen, in addition to Plato, Donnelly, and Cayce, an extensive occult literature has grown up concerning Atlantean migrations, which differs in important respects from the Cayce readings. It is worth emphasizing here what the readings did *not* say, since popular conceptions of the Atlantis story are often mistaken for the Cayce version.

The Cayce readings had a lot to say about migrations of Atlanteans to Egypt, Yucatan in Central America, and Peru in South America. The readings discuss Atlantean involvement in building pyramids in Egypt, but do not say that Atlanteans carried pyramids to Yucatan, or that they built pyramids themselves. The readings also do not say that the Atlanteans were the first people to settle in Egypt, Peru, or Yucatan. There were already thriving civilizations in place, although the arrival of the Atlanteans had a major impact. The idea of Donnelly and others that these cultures sprang full-blown without antecedents gets no support from either science or the Cayce readings.

The readings also do not say that the Atlanteans were responsible for the classic Maya or Inca civilizations, or directly for the Mound Builders of North America. Their *descendants* became these civilizations, a far different point of view. In fact, despite considerable scientific knowledge of the classical civilizations, even in Cayce's time, the readings are usually worded to indicate that he was not talking about the historically known civilizations. With rare exceptions, his Yucatan is pre-Maya, as his Peru is pre-Inca.

Now let's look at what Cayce specifically said. We will compare this with scientific opinion in his own time, and with recent scientific discoveries.

At the time of each destruction, and particularly for the last destruction, Cayce referred to migrations from Atlantis. These migrations were to the lands bordering Atlantis, including the Americas, Europe, and Egypt:

Evidences of this lost civilization are to be found in the Pyrenees and Morocco on the one hand, British Honduras, Yucatan and America on the other. (no. 364–3, February 16, 1932)

Hence . . . establishments in the Yucatan, in the Luzon, in what became the Inca, in the North American land, and in what later became known as the land of the Mound Builders in Ohio. (no. 1215–4, June 4, 1937)

The entity was among those who set sail for the Egyptian land but entered into the Pyrenees, and what is now the Portuguese, French, and Spanish lands. And there still may be seen in the chalk cliff there in Calais the marks made by the entity's followers . . . (no. 315–4, June 18, 1934)

We will first look at the migrations to the New World, then at Europe, and defer Egypt to the next chapter. The Cayce readings gave specific dates for migrations from Atlantis: 50,772 B.C. (no. 262–39, February 21, 1933); 28,000 B.C. (no.

470–22, July 5, 1938); and a range of dates between 10,000 B.C. and 11,000 B.C. in a large number of readings for the final destruction. We have seen that there is some geological support for major earth changes near these dates. Is there any evidence that people existed this long ago in the Americas, and that there were major migrations at the times given by Cayce?

Archaeology in Cayce's Time

The American archaeological mainstream in the 1920s was led by Dr. Aleš Hrdlička, curator at the U.S. National Museum at the Smithsonian Institution in Washington, D.C. Hrdlička's position was that human beings were relatively recent arrivals in North America, not more than 2,000 to 3,000 years ago. People were thought to have arrived by boat from Asia across the Bering Strait, long after the glaciers had melted. Native Americans were thought to be entirely Mongolian in origin, despite wide variations in physical types noted by many early explorers. Hrdlička's views held sway for three decades, according to archaeologist Jesse Jennings in *Prehistory of North America*, and American scholars gave no serious consideration to the possibility that the occupancy of the Americas was anything but recent. Indeed, no real evidence existed to contradict this view.

Meanwhile, the Cayce readings in 1923 said the following: ". . . we find [the entity] in that fair country of Alta or Poseidia proper . . . This we find nearly ten thousand years before the Prince of Peace came" (no. 288–1, November 20, 1923); and in 1925: ". . . we find [the entity] in the plains country of now northern and western Arizona, when the peoples were ruling in that land by the rule of settling from the Atlantean country" (no. 4211–1, June 16, 1925).

The first serious challenge to the Hrdlička viewpoint came in 1926, three years *after* Cayce's first mention of 10,000 B.C., very close to the location specified for Atlantean settlement. Near the town of Folsom, New Mexico, a cowboy named George McJunkin found stone spear points together with the bones of large bison that had become extinct in roughly 8000 B.C. Other archaeologists made similar finds, and soon these

Folsom points were proof that people had lived in North America prior to 1000 B.C. Yet, even in 1928, Hrdlička was still maintaining his position.

In 1932, near Clovis, New Mexico, yet another find confirmed human antiquity in North America. These Clovis spear points, older than the Folsom points, suggested that people had been here as far back as 10,000 B.C. The most likely route was across the Bering Strait, this time over the land bridge from Siberia to Alaska caused by the lowered sea level from the glaciers. Acceptance of these dates came nearly ten years and hundreds of readings after Cayce had originally said that people had migrated from Atlantis in 10,000 B.C. Cayce was not credited with inspiring the change in opinion, however, despite the fact that in at least six readings before 1934 he gave the same 10,000 B.C. date for migrations from Atlantis to America. Few archaeologists had probably even heard of the Cayce readings.

Prior to Cayce's time, the theories of the origin of New World racial types were speculative. Popular views included sources ranging from Atlanteans to Jews to Vikings. In the scientific community, Hrdlička's view of exclusively Asian origin dominated. By 1933, however, opinion was shifting. Earnest Hooton of Harvard University pointed out that, although the Indians are homogeneous in a number of characteristics, they differ widely in others. Hooton remarked in 1940, in a chapter of the book *The Maya and Their Neighbors*, that Mayan skeletons from a well at the site of Chichen Itza in the Yucatan were not very different from Middle Eastern skeletons of the Old World, and were not very Mongoloid. The diversity could be explained either as differentiation out of a single type that entered the New World (that is, the Mongoloid type), or as the perpetuation of existing varieties among several original groups of immigrants (this would be consistent with the Cayce Atlantis story, as well as with other explanations), W. W. Howells of the University of Wisconsin reviewed the status of this idea in another chapter of the same book, and felt that the bulk of the evidence pointed to a primarily Asian racial type. He noted, however, that especially in Native Americans of the eastern United States, evidence also points to affinities with the white racial type. Thus, even during Cayce's lifetime, opinion had begun to change.

In the following years, to Cayce's death in 1945 and beyond, numerous findings clustered between 10,000 and 9,000 B.C. convinced most archaeologists that people had entered the New World in this time frame and spread rapidly. Although these dates closely matched Cayce's, no older sites to confirm Cayce's tales of earlier migrations had been found; and Atlantis as a possible site of human origin was not seriously considered.

The Current Evidence

Modern dating methods, combined with continued excavation of sites, have led to a completely new picture of early human occupation of the New World. We can summarize only a small part of the key evidence here.

Before the 1970s, and indeed in some opinions into the 1980s, the Clovis spear points were thought to be the oldest evidence of human beings in the New World. They are now reliably dated to about 12,000 years ago (10,000 B.C.). Where did the people who made the Clovis points come from? The prevailing wisdom holds that they had come over the Bering Strait from Siberia to Alaska on a land bridge that existed at a time when the sea level had been lowered by the glaciers. The climate in that area was inhospitable, but no other means of access to the New World was apparent, and the land bridge was known to be open 12,000 years ago.

The most popular theory was that of Paul Martin, who proposed that human beings entered the New World in a migration from Asia across the Bering Strait in about 10,000 B.C., and expanded rapidly in population, causing the extinction of the large animals roaming America at that time. This has been called the "overkill hypothesis." It comes from the observation that in the same time frame, we find both a sharp increase in the number of ancient human sites and a sharp drop in the population of large animals. The Cayce readings give some support to the idea that people had planned the extinction of large animals, but they also say that climatic change was largely responsible for the earlier extinction near 50,000 B.C.

(no. 5249–1, June 12, 1944). This climate-change theory also receives some scientific support, and the debate continues between Martin and others in a book called *Quaternary Extinctions: A Prehistoric Revolution*, as to whether climate or people hastened the extinctions. Still, as recently as the early 1970s, few questioned the 10,000 B.C. date for people's first entry into North America.

By 1976, this 10,000 B.C. barrier was beginning to crumble. Richard S. MacNeish, director of the Peabody Museum of Archaeology in Massachusetts, wrote an article in *American Scientist* summarizing the numerous recently discovered more ancient sites, which ranged all the way to the tip of South America. This suggested that people had entered the New World prior to 12,000 years ago. The hitch was that, for much of this time, there was no Bering Strait land bridge. Jesse Jennings points out in *Prehistory of North America* that the only other time the Bering Strait could have been land was during the middle of the last Ice Age (about 28,000 B.C.), or before the last Ice Age even began (about 70,000 B.C.). If not over the Bering Strait, how did people *first* enter the New World? The answer from the Cayce readings, of course, is that they migrated there from Atlantis—from the east, rather than the west.

Is there any scientific evidence that people could have arrived across the Atlantic, perhaps even from Atlantis? The majority opinion holds this possibility unlikely, since ample evidence indicates that some people, such as the Eskimos, have recently come across the Bering Strait. But with the large number of ancient dates, it has become increasingly difficult to find previous land bridges in the ancient time frames required. In 1963, anthropologist E. F. Greenman proposed an idea far more consistent with the Atlantis explanation.

Greenman, an anthropology professor from the University of Michigan, argued in an article published in *Current Anthropology* that people had reached the New World from Europe by boat! He found many cultural similarities between Stone Age peoples in Europe and North America. His imposing catalog of similarities included both artwork and stone artifacts, such as spear points. Here we have evidence for transatlantic diffusion of technology, in exactly the time frame given by Cayce. This is not Mayan or Egyptian high technology, but simple stone tools. Still, for Paleolithic peoples, it was a cultural revolution. This technology could have been all that survived from the migrations of a collapsing civilization. Cayce specified the Pyrenees as another location to which Atlanteans fled, and this and other European areas are the sources for Greenman's parallels. This evidence is much more consistent with Cayce than with Donnelly's parallels between the Maya and the Egyptians. Of course, Greenman does not mention Atlantis; travel across the Atlantic by boat, perhaps along the edge of the icecap, was his best guess; but the evidence is certainly consistent with the Atlantis hypothesis.

The best evidence that people were present in the New World back at the time of the *earlier* Atlantis destruction is the large number of key sites, and the fact that more are being found and dated every year. The oldest dates are still quite controversial, but there are several well-accepted dates older than 12,000 years. The MacNeish article summarizes the sites found before 1976, and a book edited by anthropologist Richard Shutler in 1983 provides an update with even more sites. Jeffrey Goodman, in his 1981 book *American Genesis*, gives a popularized account that tries to establish that modern people appeared in America *before* other areas of the world. Though he may not have completely succeeded in that aim, he does provide a detailed guide to the evidence for early human residence in America. As with all attempts to fit psychic evidence with archaeology, Goodman's work has been criticized by skeptics. Anthropologists Marshall McKusick, in *Archaeology*, and Ken Feder, in *Skeptical Inquirer*, have attacked the entire concept of psychic archaeology, and the Goodman books and Cayce readings in particular. The reader will have to judge personally which sources present the most reasonable point of view.

One major site archaeologists feel has been validly dated is the Pikimachay Cave at Ayacucho, Peru. Peru was mentioned in numerous Cayce readings as the destination of Atlanteans in the earlier destructions. Richard MacNeish has dated layers with artifacts to 14,500 years ago; the artifacts were found in association with many bones of extinct mammals. MacNeish feels that people probably occupied the area at least as far back as twenty thousand years ago.

One of the best sites in North America is the Meadowcroft Rock Shelter in southwest Pennsylvania. As the depths of the shelter were excavated, archaeologists led by James Adovasio of the University of Pittsburgh recovered over 400 stone artifacts from a level dated at 15,000 years ago from charcoal in a fireplace. These included slender "bladelike" items similar to those found at European Cro-Magnon sites. From an even deeper level came a radiocarbon date from a possible basketry fragment of over 17,000 years ago. Adovasio's work was published in *American Antiquity* in 1977.

In an even more recent discovery, reported by Bruce Bower in *Science News* in 1986, a rock shelter in Brazil known as Pedra Furada has been radiocarbon dated to 32,000 years ago. A hearth in the shelter dated at 17,000 years ago contains a rock with two red painted lines, suggesting that cave art began in the Americas about the same time it appeared in Europe and Africa. The walls and ceilings of Pedra Furada are still covered with prehistoric paintings.

Other, more controversial sites argue for even earlier dates. The Hueyatlaco site in Mexico may be as old as 250,000 years. Virginia Steen-McIntyre of the U.S. Geological Survey showed in 1981 that layers containing artifacts were 250,000 years old. A date this old was hard for archaeologists to accept, since it was ten times older than any other date in the Americas. The debate in the journal *Quaternary Research* is ongoing.

Even more ancient, and more controversial, is the Calico Hills site in California, excavated by Louis Leakey (*Science*, 1970). Leakey's estimate for the age of the stone tools from the Calico Hills site is as much as 500,000 years! Such a concept was unthinkable to other archaeologists, who quickly came up with the alternative explanation that the stone tools were simply naturally weathered rocks. Vance Haynes of the University of Arizona has been a major proponent of the natural geological artifact theory, and this is now the most commonly held belief (*Science*, 1973). Leakey died soon after excavating the site, and was unable to carry on the debate. The site remains controversial; but, as with the Hueyatlaco site, the controversy is between mainstream archaeologists, not between science and the occult.

For the Cayce story, the evidence is quite consistent. A major population explosion, in conjunction with a pole shift, climatic change, and extinction of large animals, occurred around 12,000 years ago, at the time of the final migration from Atlantis. Evidence of early human occupation prior to this date exists not only in the Southwest, where it had been found in Cayce's time; some of the oldest remains have been found in Mexico, South America, and the eastern United States (western Pennsylvania), other locations given by Cayce for migrations from Atlantis. Richard Shutler's conclusion in 1983 was that the most significant recent advancement in early human archaeology is that we can now place the minimum time for the first occupation of North America at least 20,000 years ago, with the possibility that it occurred as long ago as 50,000 years. Archaeologists in Cayce's time would not have even thought of looking for ancient people in these locations or in this time frame. Whether or not the first Americans came over the Bering Strait or from Atlantis is a question still to be answered; but the Cayce statements, and especially his dates, are certainly no longer outside the realm of science as they were in his time.

What happened to the Atlanteans after their flight from Atlantis? Cayce's answers, when taken literally, provide little support for the Donnelly and occultist views, but are consistent with some recent scientific evidence.

Migrations to the Yucatan

Forty-one Cayce readings mention the Yucatan area of Central America, most in connection with migrations from Atlantis. When asked to give a historical treatise on the origin and development of the Maya civilization, Cayce responded, "Yes. In giving a record of the civilization in this particular portion of the world, it should be remembered that more than one has been and will be found as research progresses . . . we would turn back to 10,600 years before the Prince of Peace came into the land of promise" (no. 5750–1, November 12, 1933). The reading continues with a description of the beginnings of a civilization in Yucatan, which was eventually to become the Maya civilization.

Still other readings mention the Yucatan. ". . . The entity was in the land now known as or called the Poseidian land, or Atlantean land, during those periods in which it was breaking up, and then the children of the Law of One (to which the entity was enjoined) journeyed from the land into portions of what is now the Yucatan land" (no. 2073–2, April 12, 1940). "The entity was among those, though, who were sent to what later became or is in the present the Yucatan land, of the Mayan experience" (no. 1599–1, May 29, 1938).

Thus the Cayce readings discuss, not the Maya as they eventually developed, but their pre-Maya origins in 10,600 B.C. Did the readings make sense according to Maya archaeology in Cayce's time? By the 1930s, Maya archaeology had made major progress since the mid-1800s, despite the continuing popularity of books like Donnelly's. Explorers had uncovered much of Maya civilization, including the three "books" that survived the Spanish, lofty pyramids, huge monuments, and even courts used for games similar to basketball.

The LePlongeon translation of the Mayan book called the *Troano Codex*, alleging Mu—the "evidence" for the Donnelly and Churchward stories—was thoroughly discredited, and about one-third of the symbols of Mayan writing could be read. Sylvanus Morley, a noted Mayan language expert, wrote in 1940 that two archaeologists, Ernst Forstemann and G. T. Goodman, had independently proved conclusively by 1900 that the *Dresden Codex* was an astrological treatise based on the sun, moon, and Venus. There was clearly no resemblance of the Mayan language to Greek, as Donnelly had stated.

In Cayce's time, the foundations from which the Maya sprang were still obscure. Archaeologist A. L. Krober summarized the state of Maya archaeology in 1940, based on evidence collected at the time Cayce was giving his readings:

> It is now generally accepted that wherever we have been able to work out continuous archaeological sequences, as in parts of Mexico and our own Southwest, these carry us back about 2000 years but no more. The older

views which placed the first discovered stages in the second millenium B.C., or even earlier, seem no longer able to withstand criticism. In Peru, also, though an absolute chronology is still altogether lacking, conservative estimates incline to see the whole course of known development as having taken place since the beginning of the Christian era. (*The Maya and Their Neighbors*)

Alfred Kidder, another prominent archaeologist, said that earlier, fundamental aspects of the origin of the Maya are still lost in antiquity. He noted that the belief in a bearded white culture hero—Quetzalcoatl of the Aztecs, Kukulkan of the Maya, Bochica of the Chibcha of Columbia, and probably also Viracocha of the Peruvian Indians—is a widespread conception, but its origin is impossible to assign to any area. Donnelly had used this white hero/god as evidence for Atlantis, but that was not the accepted explanation either in Cayce's time or now.

If Cayce had intended to support Donnelly's theories, he wasn't even close to the accepted time frame in his day.

How has our knowledge of the Maya changed since Cayce's time? Have scientific discoveries made the readings' story more or less likely? Once again, modern methods of dating, combined with extensive excavation, have revealed much about the history of the Maya. In this case, there is little to confirm Cayce directly, since only a few potentially very ancient sites like Hueyatlaco have been found. The readings refer to a period of time long before the major Maya monuments that excite the fantasies of the public. Yet what the readings do say is at least not inconsistent with the findings of archaeology.

Gordon Willey, in a chapter in *Social Progress in Maya History* in 1977, discussed the progress in Maya archaeology since 1940. By 1977, the earliest date for early preclassic Maya had been pushed back to about 2000 B.C. The first construction of large ceremonial centers began after 300 B.C. The classic civilization flowered between A.D. 300 and 900. By the time the Spaniards arrived with Cortes in 1541, the Maya had been long in decline. A more recent article by Willey, published in *Science* in 1982, cites evidence gathered by Richard

MacNeish for even earlier pre-Maya inhabitants going back to 9000 B.C. It is no longer thought that the Maya appeared full-blown. Furthermore, this evidence was found in Belize, formerly British Honduras, a location on the south side of the Yucatan peninsula specifically given in reading no. 364–3 in 1932. Although there was substantial migration in and out of the area, the pre-Maya can now be traced back almost to the time given by Cayce.

We can find further evidence of consistency in the Cayce time frame in his description of the climate: "Rather than being a tropical area it was more of the temperate . . ." (no. 5750–1, November 12, 1933). Our knowledge of the climates in the area in 10,000 B.C. confirms this statement. The glaciers were still melting, and all of North America was substantially colder than it is now.

This has been indirect evidence of the consistency and plausibility of the Cayce story. But the readings contain a clue that could confirm the Cayce story of Atlantis itself, as well as the Maya. He referred to a buried temple of records, in which information on the construction of the "firestone" or "great crystal" would be found: "In Yucatan there is emblem of same [the firestone]. Let's clarify this, for it may be the more easily found—for they will be brought to this America, these United States. A portion is to be carried, as we find, to the Pennsylvania State Museum. A portion is to be carried to the Washington preservations of such findings, or to Chicago" (no. 440–5, December 19, 1933). When asked, "Who is conducting this work in Yucatan?", the reading continued, "Would it be sent to any other place than to those who were carrying on same?"

Has anything been found? Many people have wished that Cayce had been clearer in some of his readings. There were indeed expeditions to the area when Cayce gave the reading in 1933, but identifying a single artifact of unknown description is quite a challenge.

Unfortunately, the readings were not specific about the nature of the artifact, or about exactly where it would be taken. "To Chicago" could mean the Field Museum of Natural History in Chicago, or anywhere else in that very large city. "The Washington preservations of such findings" probably meant the Smithsonian, but there are other archaeological collections in Washington.

The "Pennsylvania State Museum" is also a problem, since there is more than one possibility. Many people assumed Cayce was referring to the University of Pennsylvania museum. Jeffrey Goodman, in his book *Psychic Archaeology*, tried to track down the Cayce reference. He found that, in 1933, the university museum *was* excavating at the site of Piedras Negras in Guatemala. The site report had much in common with Cayce's description; there were superimpositions of several different periods, and the site investigator, Dr. Linton Satterthwaite, said that he was "tempted to see a mixture of Mayan and non-Mayan styles." Was this the site Cayce described? Perhaps, but the library at the Association for Research and Enlightenment has photographs and a catalog from the William Penn Memorial Museum in Harrisburg, showing other archaeological digs in Yucatan, with unidentified people, dating from the 1930s. This museum was *formerly* called the Pennsylvania State Museum. Nothing has been found yet that looks like the emblem of the firestone, however.

Migrations to Peru

Cayce gave seventy-three readings mentioning incarnations in Peru, ranging from before the destruction of Atlantis up until the Spaniards conquered the Incas. The historical periods seem to be consistent in the readings—he doesn't mix Spaniards and Atlanteans! His Incas, like his Maya, come much after the destruction of Atlantis. Prior to the Atlanteans, Peru was inhabited by a people called the Ohlms or Ohums: "In the one before this, we find in that land known as the Peruvian, during the period of the Ohlms, before the Incas and the peoples of the Poseidian land entered" (no. 1916–5, January 19, 1931). "In the experience the entity was a priestess, in those interpretations of what later became known as the Incals, the Lost Tribes, the people from the Atlantean land, the peoples who came west from the activities in the Lemurian land" (no. 1159–1, May 5, 1936).

What do we know about the Incas and their origin? Anthropologist Loren McIntyre described their civilization in a book for *National Geographic* in 1975. The Incas themselves are not at all ancient. The first Inca emperor, Pachacuti, began his quest for empire in about A.D. 1438. At its greatest extent, the Inca empire spanned 2,500 miles, similar in size to the Roman empire. In 1532, the Spaniard Francisco Pizarro captured the Inca Atahualpa; this act shattered the empire at the height of its power.

It is the predecessors of the Incas who are of interest here. Richard MacNeish, discussed earlier in connection with ancient dates, has made a study of early peoples in Peru published in *Scientific American*. The Ayacucho valley high in the Andes in Peru has evidence of human occupation going back in an unbroken sequence that spans the millenniums from 20,000 B.C. to A.D. 1500. There is a progression from early hunter, to farmer, to subject of imperial rule. Deep in a cave, MacNeish found an assemblage of rather crude stone tools he called the Paccaicasa complex, after a nearby village. The people who fashioned these distinctive tools occupied the Ayacucho valley from as much as 22,000 years ago to about 13,000 years ago. Were these the Ohlms? Stone tools cannot provide the richness of detail we need to completely evaluate the Cayce readings, but once again we see that Cayce's statements about the predecessors of the Incas are not without some scientific support.

The readings speak of a later time in Peruvian history as well, but still before the arrival of the Spaniards: ". . . in the land that now may be called the Peruvian, during those periods when there were the persecutions—not those known in the much later date as from the Spaniards, but rather from the breaking up from the meeting with those from the Mayan or Yucatan land" (no. 1637–1, July 12, 1938).

Even in Cayce's time, it was recognized that the Maya had penetrated into South America, and that substantial cultural interchange had taken place. Samuel Lothrop, in 1940, discussed the diversity of opinion on exactly which cultural traits were exchanged. Some authors (Max Uhle is cited by Lothrop as an example) felt that *all* manifestations of Andean culture were derived from Middle America, for the most part as a result of actual migration. It is certainly reasonable that one result of cultural contact was persecution by invaders from Yucatan, as Cayce said.

The readings also speak of a destruction of Peru before the destruction of Atlantis, in a time when the Ohlms were the civilization: "In the one [life] before this we find in the days of the peoples coming from the waters in the submerged areas of the Southern portion as is now of Peru . . ." (no. 470–2, May 15, 1925). "In the one [life] before this, we find in the now Peruvian country, when the people were destroyed in the submerging of the land. The entity then in that of the next to the ruler in the Ohlm rule" (no. 2903–1, June 26, 1925).

As we have seen, geologists in general do not favor theories of catastrophic submergences. Surprisingly, however, there is actually some evidence of deep submergence off the coast of Peru, and even some possible sunken ruins. Dr. Robert Menzies, director of Duke University's Oceanographic Program, was reported in the *New York Times*, April 17, 1966, and in *Science World*, April 15, 1966, to have discovered carved rock columns resting on a muddy plain 6,000 feet underwater, off the coast of Peru. Menzies and his colleagues were looking for neoplinia, a type of sea mollusk, one of the earth's oldest "living fossils." Their dredges brought up some of the desired specimens, but their deep-sea diving cameras showed photographic evidence of the columns, covered with what appeared to be some sort of writing. Menzies is quoted as saying that although "the idea of a sunken city in the Pacific seems incredible, the evidence so far suggests one of the most exciting discoveries of the century." We haven't been able to find any later reports confirming or refuting this discovery, and it is hard to tell whether it was ever taken seriously by scientists. It was certainly made by a respectable researcher.

Migrations to North America

The Cayce readings mention people in North America as far back as 10 million years ago. The most ancient scientific evidence found thus far, that of Leakey at Calico Hills, possibly goes back 500,000 years, but has not been generally accepted. Most of the readings speak of much later migrations during the time of the Atlantean destructions.

Perhaps the thorniest problem with the idea of Atlantean migrations from the point of view of anthropologists is that most of the evidence points to the descent of the Native American population from immigrants over the Bering Strait. Despite cultural parallels with Europe, such as those of Greenman, Native Americans appear to be most closely related genetically to Asians. What does this do to the Cayce story?

The readings acknowledge a complex mixture of immigrants to America: "... the entity was in the land of the present nativity [Nebraska] during those periods when there were activities in separating the peoples in the southland from those coming in from the western lands or from the isles of the sea" (no. 3179–1, August 26, 1943).

Robert Wauchope, in *Lost Tribes and Sunken Continents*, has discussed extensively all the "crackpot" theories of the origin of the Native Americans. Long before Cayce, dating back to the 1700s, many wild theories were popular. It is difficult not to place oneself in their company by even bringing up the topic. Clearly, Cayce's audience would have been familiar with some of these ideas. Is there any support *at all* for the idea that the Native Americans may have had multiple origins; that they did not simply arrive over the Bering Strait, but from Africa, Europe, or even Atlantis? The Cayce readings seem to reflect these speculations, and mention both the Lost Tribes and an Atlantean origin for the Mound Builders: "The entity was among the first of those of the second generation of Atlanteans who struggled northward from Yucatan, settling in what is now a portion of Kentucky, Indiana, Ohio; being among those of the earlier period known as Mound Builders" (no. 3528–1, December 20, 1943).

The Mound Builders, a term loosely applied to cultures called Adena, Hopewell, and Mississippian by archaeologists, were the inhabitants of eastern and midwestern America from roughly 1000 B.C. to A.D. 1673, when the first French explorers arrived. The "mounds" are large earthworks, often used for burials. The most famous mound is the Cahokia mound in Illinois, 100 feet tall. The earthworks of the Mound Builders, although not as impressive as the Pyramids of Yucatan, were thought by early explorers to be beyond the capability of the "primitive" local Indians. Robert Silverberg, in his book *The*

Mound Builders, discusses the many fanciful theories of their origin, including the idea that Atlanteans or even Danish Vikings had built the mounds. Carbon-14 dating has shown that the mounds were built by the immediate ancestors of the Native Americans, and some were even built after the Europeans arrived. But this doesn't solve the problem of the *origin* of the Mound Builders. How long had they been there, and where did they come from?

The Cayce readings tell us, not that the Atlanteans were the Mound Builders, but that their descendants were. A site called Koster in Illinois reveals the people that became the Mound Builders, and provides a record of a sophisticated culture that goes back almost to the time of the Cayce Atlanteans.

Anthropologist Stuart Streuver of Northwestern University, directing the excavation of this site, was amazed to find layer after layer of ancient occupations, over 30 feet thick and dating back over 9,000 years. Prior to this discovery, people assumed that, for most of their history, the Native Americans had been primitive nomadic hunter-gatherers. But at Koster, Streuver found evidence of sophisticated construction of buildings, possibly including plaster walls, going back thousands of years. The builders of the famous mounds were not the first advanced culture in the area, merely the most visible. According to Streuver, people were in the area as early as 9500 B.C. He feels the later Mound Builders are descended from these early arrivals, since the later skeletons at Koster are very similar to the early ones. The evidence tends to refute Donnelly, but to support Cayce. Although some later cultural input from Central America influenced the construction of the mounds in later years, the original settlers could indeed have been "of the second generation of Atlanteans."

Has any evidence been found that would support Cayce by showing that these original ancestors of the Mound Builders arrived from the south, rather than from the west, after crossing the Bering Strait? One of the more interesting pieces of evidence consistent with the Cayce story of Atlanteans in North America comes from linguistics. The readings said, "The entity then was among the people, the Indians, of the Iroquois; those of noble birth, those that were of the pure descendants of the Atlanteans" (no. 1219–1, July 13, 1936).

A recent linguistic study in a 1985 *Quaternary Research* by Richard Rogers, an anthropologist from the University of Kansas, suggests that, before 18,000 years ago, when the glaciers covered much of North America, there was already a linguistically distinct population in the southeast. As the glaciers melted, near the time of the final destruction of the Cayce Atlantis, the people migrated northward. Their linguistic family, Algonquian, is distinct from the languages of the west. Iroquoian, another eastern language family, is also not related to the languages of the west. The article does not discuss the Atlantean theory, but at the very least it shows that Native Americans are not descended from a single population that came over the Bering Strait in 10,000 B.C.

Once again, the scientific evidence puts Cayce in a relatively good light. Whatever their origin, it appears that these people entered the region in the time frame given by Cayce, and eventually became the Mound Builders. For thousands of years, their culture was at a higher level than anyone had thought possible. This evidence does not directly support the Atlantis *origin*, but is consistent with it.

Are Native Americans descended from any race other than Asian? The answer is not simple. Even if there is evidence for more than one racial input, this can be explained by postulating successive waves of migration over the Bering Strait. Some of these migrations may have included ancestors of modern Caucasians who crossed Asia.

Cayce himself brings up one of the other problems with finding the Atlantean influence in Native American races: later transatlantic migration. The readings refer to the "Lost Tribes." One of the popular theories, not taken seriously by most anthropologists, was that Native Americans were the descendants of the "lost tribes of Israel" captured in the eighth century B.C. by the king of Assyria. A related theory comes from the Book of Mormon. The Mormons believe in two other migrations of Jews to America.

Cayce was not specific as to what he meant by the Lost Tribes. Although no scientists today believe that the Jews were literally the major ancestors of the Native Americans, there is some evidence for transatlantic contact. Scientists continue to debate how important that contact was, or whether it was necessary to account for cultural parallels.

Thor Heyerdahl is one of the major proponents of transatlantic diffusion. Heyerdahl is a Norwegian explorer who has sailed primitive craft across the oceans to prove that ancient people could have done it as well. In 1970, he sailed the *Ra II* from North Africa to the Caribbean. *Ra II* was a reed boat, similar to those used both in Africa and in Lake Titicaca in South America. In *Early Man and the Oceans*, Heyerdahl chronicles the history of diffusionist thinking, and lists a variety of cultural traits that he feels are best explained by diffusion. These include some of Donnelly's parallels; but Heyerdahl feels that they are due to contact across the ocean, not to Atlantis. They are consistent with the Cayce readings, however, which describe a time

> . . . during that period as would be called 3,000 years before the Prince of Peace came, those peoples that were of the Lost Tribes, a portion came into the land.
> [Q-1.] How did the Lost Tribe reach this country?
> [A-1.] In boats. (no. 5750–1, November 12, 1933)

Heyerdahl notes that shortly before 3000 B.C., exceptional cultural activity took place in the inner Mediterranean, with new dynasties suddenly coming into power and building up advanced local civilizations in Mesopotamia and in Egypt. He correlates this with the zero year in the ancient Mayan calendar of 3113 B.C., and suggests that it is evidence of transatlantic contact.

Ivan Van Sertima is another diffusionist. In *They Came Before Columbus*, he also makes a case that "tribes" from Africa arrived in Central America by boat. The evidence includes Olmec stone sculptures and numerous Mayan carvings showing Negroid and Semitic features. Much of Van Sertima's evidence comes from the work of Alexander von Wuthenau, professor of Mexican art history at the University of the Americas in Mexico City. His thirty-five years of work produced hundreds of examples of other racial groups in Mayan art.

These diffusionist views are not in the mainstream of archaeology. Most of the anthropology done on the racial characteristics of Native Americans has focused on the western side of the continent and the Pacific Rim. It is clear that the Eskimos and the natives of the northwest United States and Canada are relatively recent immigrants from Asia. Christy Turner has shown, based on tooth anatomy, that there is a substantial Asian component to the Native Americans of Central and South America as well. Perhaps the original Atlantean genetic contribution was swamped by later immigrants from Asia. But there has been little focus on work that could support the Cayce story. Comparisons around the Atlantic rim will be necessary to fully test Cayce's concepts.

The Cayce readings are unique in that they reconcile both the diffusionist and the Atlantean views in their proper time frames, with specific dates given well before these dates were known to archaeologists. Whether either view will eventually become compatible with mainstream science is another question, but the groundwork appears to have been laid. The debate is on a scientific level, rather than occult speculation.

Migrations to Europe

Before we proceed to the details of actual expeditions to Egypt and Bimini, let's take a brief look at the migrations to the eastern side of the Atlantic: the European area near the Pyrenees in France and Spain. As noted earlier, Europe is the area in which Cro-Magnon man, the first appearance of anatomically modern people, was discovered. This sudden appearance with a culture far higher than that of the Neanderthals has been cited by virtually every Atlantis writer since Donnelly. Do we know any more that would tend to confirm or refute the Cayce readings?

The area of southern France, Spain, and Portugal, and specifically the Pyrenees mountains on the border between Spain and France, was given in several Cayce readings as a major location to which Atlanteans fled. In some readings, it was given as a way station on the trip to Egypt.

Another reading mentioned the chalk cliffs at Calais (no. 315–4, June 18, 1934). This reference is an example of the type of discrepancy that occasionally appears in the transcriptions of the Cayce readings (which were taken down as dictation) and complicates their study. Calais is a well-known area in France, but it is not near the Pyrenees. Gladys Davis Turner, who stenographed the readings, thought later that Cayce may have been referring to another location. A French A.R.E. member pointed out that an area of Spain near Portugal and the Pyrenees is named Galice or Galicia, and that the two words rhyme. Galicia or Galice is located in northern Spain, where all of Cayce's other readings placed the migrating Atlanteans, and has cliffs and mountainous terrain. Calais, on the other hand, has flat terrain and is located 600 miles away in France bordering on the English channel.

The area of northern Spain and the Pyrenees is well known as a rich source of archaeological finds. According to archaeologist L. G. Straus, in a recent review article on the prehistory of northern Spain in *Science*, this area is considered to be one of the best sources of information on human physical and cultural evolution. Research has been going on steadily since the 1870s, when rock art was discovered in an Altamira cave by M. Sanz de Sautola. Virtually all known sites from the time Cayce gave for Atlantis are in caves; open-air sites have either been eroded or deeply buried.

Neanderthal man is represented in several sites, and lasts until about 35,000 years ago. There is little evidence of art or adornment at this time, and technology appears to have been limited to very simple stone and bone tools.

Some major changes begin to appear about 35,000 years ago, with the onset of the period known as the Upper Paleolithic and the appearance of anatomically modern people. Although technology was still Stone Age, this was a time of growth in the roles of technology, social organization, and planning. Tools became far more sophisticated. There is substantial evidence of human construction activity about 29,000 years ago in a site called Cueva Morin, including a large dugout feature, postholes, and graves with possible offerings.

Well-dated cultures in the late Upper Paleolithic—the Solutrean from 20,500 to 17,000 years ago and the Magdalenian from 17,000 to 11,000 years ago—show great development in both the well-known cave art and specialized technologies such as the spear-thrower and the arrow. More than sixty caves with cave art have been discovered in the area. The people also developed elaborate uses of fire.

The transition to the Mesolithic, or Middle Stone Age, comes around 11,000 years ago, near the time of the final destruction of Atlantis. As we have seen in North America, there were major climate changes, the growth of new forests, and the rising of sea levels. The Neolithic, which we often think of as paving the way for civilization—with pottery and domesticated animals, began around 5,000 years ago, long after the sinking of Atlantis.

It is hard to make a case for or against Atlantis from what we know in Europe. On the one hand, in the Cayce time frame there were major cultural advancements in Europe that in many cases appear to have been brought in from outside. Greenman's evidence for cultural parallels with North America suggests transatlantic contact. On the other hand, as in North America, these were Stone Age technologies, not the high technologies spoken of by Cayce. Perhaps all that survived the destruction of a civilization was the basic knowledge and intelligence, but not the means to rebuild.

We have seen in this chapter that geologists and archaeologists completely unaware of the Cayce readings have in many cases come up independently with supporting evidence. Yet, because Cayce was considered a psychic, his readings weren't used to guide research. Many questions have been raised by the readings that have simply never been addressed scientifically. A concerted effort has never been made to find Atlantean ruins on the mid-Atlantic ridge. Most of the evidence supporting even the possibility of Atlantis has been found accidentally, and scientists are quite right in saying that it is ambiguous.

What would it take to prove Cayce right or wrong? Where would researchers have the best chance of finding evidence of Atlantis? These same questions were asked in Cayce's day, and the readings were quite specific. Records of Atlantis would be found in three places: Egypt, Bimini, and Yucatan. Cayce's listeners in the 1930s missed their chance to track down evidence from Yucatan as it was carried to the United States. But the next two chapters follow the explorers who, inspired by the Cayce readings, have taken the search to Egypt and Bimini, and who may, perhaps, lead us to Atlantis.

Part III

QUESTS FOR EVIDENCE

5

THE SEARCH IN EGYPT

ANCIENT EGYPT: THE Sphinx, the Great Pyramid, and temples covered with hieroglyphics. The very size and grandeur of these enigmatic structures create awe and stimulate interest, leading to questions by serious researchers and curious laypeople alike. Who built them? Why? How? What ancient culture was capable of designing and constructing them? For centuries, archaeologists have attempted to answer these questions, resulting in conflicting theories and views—none satisfactory to every school of thought.

But what do questions about Egypt and its archaeological wonders have to do with Edgar Cayce and Atlantis? The stories of Atlantis and Egypt are intertwined in the Cayce readings. In life readings mentioning Atlantis, Cayce often detailed locations where individuals fled during the final destruction. Among other areas, he repeatedly designated Egypt as one of the major destinations of the fleeing Atlanteans. The readings also say that one of Edgar Cayce's most important incarnations was as an Egyptian priest and leader named Ra-Ta or Ra, and occurred during this time frame. Many people receiving life readings were said to have been associated with him in this past life. Finally, throughout this material, references and clues indicate Egypt as a repository for records—records of Atlantis and ancient Egypt during the time of Ra-Ta, which may someday be found. They also mention again and again tombs and pyramids ''yet to be uncovered'' in Egypt, and give specific dates for building the Great Pyramid of Giza.

Yet the story of Egypt Cayce depicts is extremely different

from current Egyptological thought. Archaeologists and Egyptologists attempting to decipher the history of Egypt have found it a formidable task due to scanty records, conflicting reports by ancient scholars, and the total destruction of the Alexandria library, as well as the pillage and destruction of Egypt's monuments and scripts. Fitting together the remains of this complicated mosaic is both intriguing and frustrating. However, conventional views all agree that the Cayce dates of 10,000 B.C. and older do not even come close to current concepts of the chronology of the reigns of the pharaohs. Most scholars consider any time before about 4000 B.C. to have been one of primitive Stone Age cultures. Egyptologist Cyril Aldred sets the beginning of the First Dynasty at approximately 3168 B.C., and assigns the construction of the Great Pyramid of Giza to Khufu or Cheops of the Fourth Dynasty around 2700 B.C. Could Egyptologists be wrong? Could some of those great ruins be the remnants of a far earlier culture, never even imagined or considered by current Egyptologists?

The Edgar Cayce Foundation (ECF), the organization responsible for preserving the Cayce readings and accumulating evidence that confirms or refutes them, took on the challenge of ancient Egypt. The purposes for the ECF's involvement in Egypt were twofold: (1) to determine if the Edgar Cayce data about Egypt and Atlantis might be valid; and (2) to discover avenues to accomplish this through sponsoring scholars and supporting archaeological research projects in Egypt.

Thus some projects were not directly related to finding the hidden chambers or the records mentioned in the readings. They either focused on other parallels possible in this data, or were worthwhile contributions to Egyptology in their own right.

This type of work in Egypt is not unique; biblical scholars and archaeologists have long struggled with a similar problem. For, according to the Bible, "Moses was learned in the wisdom of the Egyptians" (Acts 7:22); and "only the wisdom of Solomon exceeded Egypt's" (I Kings 4:29–31). Yet Egyptian texts have no record of the biblical characters Moses or Joseph, nor of the story of the Exodus or many of the other events that comprise the historical basis of the Jewish and Christian faiths. Archaeologists cannot even identify with certainty which pharaoh the Bible describes in these particular periods. However, the Bible receives support from many other sources, and no doubt the search to validate its history archaeologically will continue.

Heinrich Schliemann's discovery of Troy in the 1870s is another example. Schliemann took Homer's writing about Troy seriously, decided to determine for sure if Homer was correct, and despite the scorn and ridicule of his contemporaries, proceeded to dig up one of the most exciting archaeological finds of his time—Troy! While his discovery eventually became a delight to archaeologists, a myth becoming a reality demanded the rearranging of past ideas.

But the Cayce readings are much more outlandish than the Bible or the story of Troy, and archaeological projects to confirm or disprove a myth are not the rule. Archaeology is the search for human history to better understand both ourselves and our culture—but searching for traces of a legendary land, based on a psychic's information? Even when scientifically approached, most professionals cringe.

Over twenty years ago, the ECF began to lay the groundwork for what would later become actual fieldwork in Egypt. The specific areas of interest were the Sphinx, the Great Pyramid, and the immediate surrounding area known as the Giza plateau. The driving force for this research was Edgar Cayce's eldest son, Hugh Lynn Cayce. Motivated by his father's psychic readings (which described his former lives in Atlantis and Egypt), as well as a personal interest in archaeology, he turned his energy and enthusiasm to initiating solid archaeological research that might validate them. It was only through the vision and energy of Hugh Lynn Cayce and his inspiration of young scholars and financial donors that this work was done.

The research the ECF became involved in during this time is in itself amazing; that it occurred at all is just as extraordinary. Much of the story lies, not in great discoveries, but in the struggle to conduct any research at all. Although some work was done by people who had little interest in the Cayce material, the majority of research came through efforts of individuals who were willing at least to examine the Cayce information and entertain ideas that challenge traditional Egyptology. Reputable organizations became willing to associate with the ECF, an unknown organization they originally viewed askance, because they realized that the ECF's main interest lay in supporting solid research relevant to the Cayce readings, not in whether the results proved the readings valid or invalid. The research to date has uncovered anomalies that may lead to changes in our concepts of Egyptian history. It has not proved Cayce correct, and in some cases argues against the Cayce story; but it has produced results that are difficult to reconcile with traditional findings, and several projects have been recognized by experts as significant contributions to Egyptology.

The first part of this chapter will look at the Cayce readings that led to this research. The second part will discuss the projects the ECF became involved with to determine the validity of the readings. For easy reference in this chapter, see Figure 5-1, which is a map of the major archaeological areas in Egypt. Figure 5-2 shows a detailed map of the Giza plateau.

RECORDS IN EGYPT?

Since time immemorial, people have sought to preserve a record of their activities: from legends and crude markings on the walls of caves, to our modern monuments and libraries. The methods have been different, but the purpose has been the same. The Sphinx and the Great Pyramid of Giza surely attest to the ancient Egyptians' attempt to preserve a record of themselves and their understandings. For the moment, assume that the Atlantis and Egypt Edgar Cayce described really did exist. It is so strange, then, to think that Atlanteans of 12,000 years ago might have wanted to preserve some record of their culture? Or that the Egyptians would want to do the same? Indeed, if Atlantean society were as technically advanced as described in the previous chapter, and they were party to such philosophical concepts about spirit, mind, and matter as the preceding chapters address, it would be almost ridiculous to assume otherwise.

When we speak of the structures on the Giza plateau, to what do we refer? The reading excerpts mention major struc-

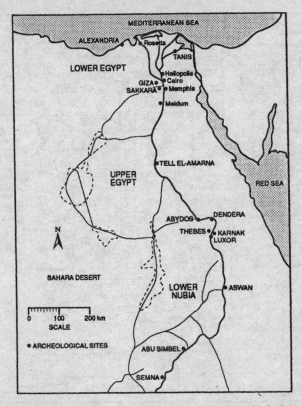

Figure 5-1. Map of Egypt, showing archaeological sites.

tures such as the Sphinx, the Great Pyramid of Giza, and pyramids and tombs yet to be uncovered in the surrounding area. Reference to Figure 5-1 will give you a quick overview of the important archaeological areas of Egypt. Giza is in the north of Egypt, near the Nile River. Figure 5-2 depicts the Giza plateau and the relative positions of the pyramids and major monuments. The Great Pyramid is the largest of three large pyramids. The Sphinx lies to the east, toward the Nile river. The area between the Sphinx and the river was largely empty

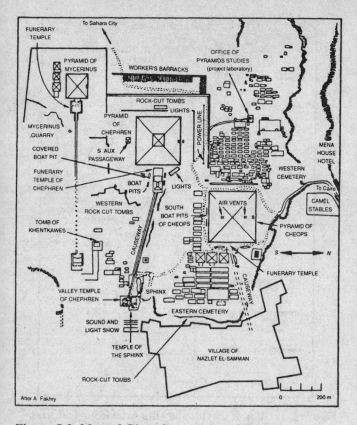

Figure 5-2. Map of Giza plateau area of Egypt.

in Cayce's time, but today it is the location of the crowded village of Nazlet el-Samman. Surrounding the three large structures are numerous smaller pyramids, tombs, and temples, many still buried beneath the sand.

Where in the Cayce readings did the ideas come from about records in Egypt? As with the Atlantis story, incidental remarks occurred over twenty years in individual life readings, as well as in a few readings given specifically on the subjects of Atlantis and Egypt.

Briefly, Cayce's Egypt story pushes active Egyptian culture back almost 12,500 years to about 10,500 B.C. It describes the original society and culture developing from various nomadic influxes of peoples to the Nile valley (from both the Carpathian mountains of Asia and from Arabia), who settled with the peoples already in Egypt and took political control. Some of these readings even indicate that this culture was actively involved in archaeological research of its own regarding *earlier* societies!

Another major external influence on the culture Cayce describes is the influx or migration to this area before and during the final destruction of Atlantis. According to Cayce's psychic data, the upper classes of the Atlantean race looked like modern people; they used the less developed "things" for servants and experimentation. In Egypt, they considered the majority of the people no higher than "menial" in physiological development, and their cultural and technical stance extremely backward.

The story of Egypt in this material revolves around how the Atlanteans handled this situation and proceeded to correct it; how the culture attempted to establish and maintain an understanding among their peoples of the relationship between human beings and the Creative Forces; and what they did to leave a record of their knowledge and history to posterity. It is beyond the scope of this book to relate all the turmoils—politically, racially, and spiritually—described in the readings, and the eventual resolution depicted in Egypt. (Refer to the A.R.E. booklet *The Egyptian Heritage* for a complete account, as well as directly to the Cayce readings.) Here we will present a sampling of reading quotes, which (1) describe the Atlantean migration to Egypt and a determination to preserve records; (2) suggest that buried pyramids and tombs may still be found in Egypt; (3) seem to describe specifically where these records are hidden; and (4) give exact dates for the structures in Egypt.

Exactly what did the Cayce readings say about an Atlantean influx into Egypt at the time of the last destruction? What remarks suggest an Atlantean connection to Egyptian culture and a preoccupation with preserving the records? According to Cayce, at the final destruction many Atlanteans knew their land was breaking up and fled both east and west. For example: "... in Atlantean land when there was knowledge that there soon was to be the destruction of that land, and there were attempts of individuals to leave the land. Entity among those who went to Egypt" (no. 708–1, October 25, 1934). "... There were evidences and prophecies of Atlantis being broken up, and Egypt was chosen as one of those places where the records of that activity were to be established" (no. 275–38, January 16, 1934).

For the Atlanteans, a major concern when migrating to Egypt was the preservation of records and their safe establishment both on the Giza plateau and elsewhere. For example, "Before that the entity was in that land now known as the Egyptian during the periods when there were those coming from the Atlantean land and bringing the records" (no. 764–1, December 18, 1934). "... for the entity was in charge of those records when the last peoples of Atlantis journeyed to the various quarters of the globe" (no. 378–13, August 14, 1933).

What did the readings say about tombs and chambers yet to be uncovered or opened in Egypt? The impression given is that much remains to be discovered in Egypt:

> ... the entity among those that were buried in the tomb or in those that are yet uncovered—yet faces the Sphinx and is nearest of those buried in that mount. (no. 1717–1, June 25, 1930)
>
> Many are the temples builded later in the plains that are yet to be uncovered near the Sphinx ... (no. 900–275, October 22, 1926)
>
> ... for the later pyramids, or those not yet uncovered ... are between the Sphinx (or the Mystery) and the Nile, or the river ... (no. 2124–3, October 2, 1931)
>
> ... the entity builded the first of the pyramids that are yet not uncovered. [Q-1.] In referring to the uncovered pyramids in the Egyptian land, near what present place are those pyramids?

[A-1.] Between that as is known as the Mystery of the Ages and the river. (no. 2124–3, October 2, 1931)

Other quotes are more specific, suggesting that these pyramids may eventually be discovered. At least one such undiscovered chamber or pyramid, according to Cayce, contains records of Atlantis: "The entity was among those that aided in the actual building of some of these buildings that still remain, and in the preparation of that one yet to be uncovered— the hall of records—where much may be brought to light" (no. 519–1, February 20, 1934).

Another reading offers more hope that this "hall of records" may someday be discovered: ". . . the entity joined with those who were active in putting records in forms that were partially of the old characters of the ancient or early Egyptian and part in the newer form of the Atlanteans. These may be found, especially when the house or tomb of records is opened, in a few years from now" (no. 2537–1, July 17, 1941).

This reading gives a general location for the record house:

. . . the activities or truths were prepared upon tablets and placed with the entity in the Tomb of Records.

[Q-7.] Where are those tablets or records made of that Egyptian experience which I might study?

[A-7.] In the Tomb of Records as indicated. For the entity's tomb then was part of the Hall of Records, which has not yet been uncovered. It lies between—or along the entrance from the Sphinx to the temple—or the pyramid, in a pyramid, of course, of its own. (no. 2329–3, May 1, 1941)

Other readings gave more specific references to chambers, pyramids, and underground tunnels beneath the paws of the Sphinx and in front of the Sphinx. There appear to be two locations of hidden records, one in the base of the Sphinx itself, and the other in a chamber that can be reached from beneath the Sphinx: "These and many findings, as given, may be found in the base of the left forearm, or leg, of the prostrate beast; in the base of the foundation. Not in the underground channel (as was opened by the ruler many years, centuries later) but in the real base, or that as would be termed in the present parlance as the cornerstone" (no. 953–24, June 12, 1926). "... was the first to set the records that are yet to be discovered or yet to be had of those activities in the Atlantean land, and for the preservation of the data, that as yet to be found from the chambers of the way between the Sphinx and the pyramid of records" (no. 1486–1, November 26, 1937).

Two other reading quotes give reasonably definite locations to search for the Hall of Records: "This in position lies, as the sun rises from the waters, the line of the shadow (or light) falls between the paws of the Sphinx, that was later set as the sentinel or guard, and which may not be entered from the connecting chambers from the Sphinx's paw (right paw) until the time has been fulfilled when the changes must be active in this sphere of man's experience" (no. 378–16, October 29, 1933). "There is a chamber or passage from the right forepaw to this entrance of the record chamber or record tomb" (no. 5748–6, July 31, 1932).

The next reading seems to indicate a relationship or plan between the Sphinx and other pyramids and buildings on the Giza plateau: [Q-6.] "In what capacity did the entity act regarding the building of the Sphinx?" [A-6.] "As the monuments were being *rebuilt* in the plains of that now called the Pyramid of Giza, this entity builded, laid, the foundations; that is superintended same, figured out the geometrical position of same in relation to those buildings as were put up of the connecting Sphinx. And the data concerning same may be found in the vaults in the base of the Sphinx" (no. 195–14, July 18, 1925).

These quotes give a date for the construction of the Great Pyramid and construction of or work on the Sphinx. They also suggest who built them:

[Q-5.] What was the date of the actual beginning and ending of the construction of the Great Pyramid?
[A-5.] Was one hundred years in construction. Begun and completed in the period of Araaraart's time, with Hermes and Ra.
[Q-6.] What was the date B.C. of that period?
[A-6.] 10,490 to 10,390 before the Prince of Peace

entered into Egypt. (no. 5748–6, July 1, 1932)

Then, with Hermes and Ra . . . there began the building of that now called Gizeh. . . . (no. 281–43, November 8, 1939)

. . . Some 10,500 years before the coming of the Christ into the land, there was first that attempt to restore and add to that which had been begun on what is called the Sphinx, and the treasure or storehouse facing same, between this and the Nile, in which those records were kept. (no. 5748–5, June 30, 1932)

From the preceding quotes, it sounds as if one might dig under the paws of the Sphinx and find a hidden pyramid. Such exploration is not so simple. The Sphinx is an Egyptian national monument. To excavate there would be akin to asking permission to dig up the foundations of the Washington Monument or Lincoln Memorial to determine if shafts or hidden chambers exist.

However, the quotes were exciting enough to inspire preparation for research in Egypt that eventually led to high-technology exploration, excavations in particular areas, and a thorough examination of the Sphinx.

These Egypt readings were all given by 1941, at a time when there was no one capable of mounting an expedition to search for the records. Egypt was only a dream to the many individuals who were told that they had past lives there. It was not until 1957 that anyone had the determination and drive to begin the search.

1957: THE QUEST BEGINS

The first research effort in Egypt was made by an adventurous and determined college student. "Rhonda James" (a pseudonym used by her request) became interested in Edgar Cayce, came to Virginia Beach, and studied many of the life readings that concerned ancient Egypt. She became curious about records that were said to be located near the Sphinx, and decided to investigate the possibility that this information might be based on fact.

No money was available from the ECF to support her research, but she was determined to go. At twenty-seven, she and a friend saved up enough money to travel to Egypt on an ocean freighter; and in the fall of 1957 they were on their way to Cairo. In retrospect, Rhonda today says that the idea of two young women heading to Egypt to prove or disprove something in the Cayce data seems preposterous. At the time, however, it seemed quite natural. Actual field investigation of the area Cayce mentioned seemed the only logical route to follow if she were to determine the information's validity and to answer her own personal questions.

Strange as it may seem, Rhonda eventually obtained permission to bore eight holes about 3 meters apart at the base of the Sphinx. They used hand-operated drills, and at about 8 feet they hit water. Despite her best efforts at the time, she discovered no chambers or passageways.

Rhonda returned to her studies and later married, but her interest in Egypt remained. She summed up her results in an unpublished twelve-page report she made to the ECF. Her observations were a precursor to extensive later work by other individuals, and their full significance will become clearer later in this chapter.

Rhonda spoke with an individual who accompanied the Egyptian archaeologist Dr. Selim Hassan years earlier when he did the most complete excavations at Giza to that date. She quotes this person in her report:

> . . . there were large limestone blocks in the rear of the body where the tail commences. These were not examined, but covered with brickwork, nor were the other blocks examined.
>
> Due east of the Sphinx, on the other side of the road leading to the Great Pyramid is a small sand hill. [The hill was investigated but the investigation did not continue far enough west.] Some blackened limestone was found, that seemed to be part of a crenulated Old Kingdom facade, which might have come from a small temple. Since there was supposed to have been a small pyramid over the spot where the record chamber was, this may or may not be indicative.

[In her summary she states that] the evidence, though slight and not conclusive, is promising. The visual evidence alone is sufficient as a basis for a thorough examination of the Sphinx for there is no known record of such. Dr. Selim Hassan in his excavation cleared the sand from the Sphinx and repaired damaged parts, but he removed no stones. There is almost no contemporary information on the Sphinx. Who built it or why is mainly conjecture. Foundation deposits containing such information were usually placed under most temples; so possibly some such might be found under one of the large limestone blocks composing the paws. Nor is there a complete study of the Sphinx, itself, available. Such a reference work is needed and would constitute a valuable contribution to Egyptology.

1973–1976: ESTABLISHING RESEARCH CONNECTIONS IN EGYPT

"It's like the beaver told the rabbit as they stared up at the immense Hoover Dam, 'No, I didn't actually build it myself. But it was based on an idea of mine.'" This statement made by Nobel Prize winner Charles H. Towne in reference to his role in laser technology applies just as aptly to the subsequent research involvement in Egypt by the Edgar Cayce Foundation, ensuing from its first move in 1973. The idea for this project came from Hugh Lynn Cayce. The ECF, through interested financial supporters, saw the long-term potential of Hugh Lynn Cayce's idea, and provided funds for implementation. The efforts and determination of a gifted individual produced the eventual results.

The first project the ECF initiated in Egypt through fiscal backing was not an actual "in-field" excavation or archaeological dig. It was a two-year academic scholarship to an individual at American University in Cairo (AUC), plus a small stipend. Hugh Lynn Cayce hoped that a "no strings attached" academic scholarship for a person who was intensely interested in Egypt and Egyptology might prove mutually advantageous to both the scholar and the ECF. The scholar could complete a degree in Cairo and gain firsthand experience with the academic community, as well as obtain field experience and make contacts in his field. For the ECF, such support could create a realistic perspective on research efforts in Egypt, produce contacts, and lead eventually to research involvement in this area. Although the scholar would be independent of the ECF, his presence in Egypt would serve as an effective liaison or channel for the ECF to develop long-term involvement there.

The ECF supported its scholar academically from 1973 to 1976, and eventually Hugh Lynn Cayce's vision and the donors' investments were justified. The student began at AUC on a non-degree "year abroad" program, switched to full-term status, and graduated in 1976 with high honors. After graduation, ECF supported him as a research fellow at AUC for several years in the department of anthropology. During this time, the student not only continued his academic studies, but also made contacts with people and organizations well known for their research in Egypt. These contacts made it possible for the ECF to sponsor—directly in some cases, and partially in others—actual field research.

Although it may sound absurd, it is sometimes difficult to spend money. Many scholars do not want their names associated with an organization whose main purpose is to preserve and study the work of a psychic. Many organizations hesitate to accept money from or have their names associated with such an organization. It was the ECF's scholar who made the contacts with individuals and organizations, and it was the recognition of his excellent fieldwork and academic prowess that earned their respect for him and the organization that was his sponsor. This was not accomplished overnight. It required over four years of effort, patience, and cooperation.

Not all of ECF's work or that of the scholar was directed at the questions raised by the Cayce readings on Atlantis and Egypt. During this time, ECF supported digs in Egypt that were worthwhile in their own right. This allowed field training for the scholar and increased his expertise. Sponsorship of these projects also increased ECF's credibility in the eyes of academics and research organizations, and helped pave the way for later work.

ECF's support of the Nag Hammadi dig at Faw Qibli, Egypt, in 1976 and 1977, is an example of one such project. Under the auspices of the Institute for Antiquity and Christianity in Claremont, California, and the direction of Dr. James Robinson, the Coptic Library in Cairo translated and published the forty-two manuscripts on Gnosticism found in the late 1940s near the town of Nag Hammadi. Concepts found in these writings about early Christians often parallel those found in the Edgar Cayce readings. The Nag Hammadi dig began after the texts were all translated and published—and occurred in the area where they were discovered.

Support of these expeditions allowed ECF's scholar to join the expedition for field training in archaeology as well as increase contacts for future networking projects. It also demonstrated the ECF's interest in worthwhile archaeological projects in Egypt.

1974 AND 1977: ARCHAEOLOGY WITHOUT A SHOVEL: USING MODERN TECHNOLOGY TO DISCOVER THE PAST

During the mid-1970s, two projects leading to contacts and eventual field research by the ECF were conducted by other researchers and funded by the National Science Foundation. As a joint effort of the Arab Republic of Egypt (Ain Shams University) and the United States (Stanford Research Institute (SRI)), research teams explored the possibilities of practically incorporating modern techniques into archaeological field research. The 1974 project applied ground-penetrating radar techniques to the pyramids of Giza and the surrounding necropolis (area of other tombs). The major purpose was to find anomalies on an archaeological site that might be indicative of hidden chambers, without disturbing the existing locale. Detection by such techniques would pinpoint exact areas for investigation before initiation of excavation.

Unfortunately, radar probing of the pyramids in search of

unknown chambers or passages in the Giza area did not succeed, due to the high porosity and poor quality of rock there and the limitations of current technology. Although this technique could only be used successfully in areas like the Sahara, where there is dry, wind-blown sand, it paved the way for work in the 1980s that would succeed in discovering hidden chambers. Meanwhile, the researchers considered other methods of investigating major Egyptological sites with this type of rock and terrain.

The 1977 project developed quite naturally out of the failure of the previous project's technique—radar—and was also funded by the National Science Foundation. It was a continuation of the previous one, but with new instrumentation. As before, the purpose was a creative attempt to incorporate modern technology into field archaeology.

However, the scope of this project was much larger. Planned investigation occurred on six noted archaeological sites in Egypt—Giza, Saqquara, Dashur, Alexandria, Tanis, and Thebes. Instead of using one sensing modality (radar in the 1974 project), they used several complementary techniques: (1) resistivity measurements, (2) magnetometry, (3) aerial photography, and (4) thermal infrared imagery.

Resistivity measurement involves driving metal rods into the earth at regular intervals to measure the ground's resistance to an electrical current. The theory is that hollows or cavities will present a high resistance to the flow of current and show up as an anomaly when resistance values are plotted. Using this method, SRI detected five anomalies—two in front of the paws of the Sphinx! Unfortunately, the Sphinx was not a planned area for investigation; SRI's survey using resistivity measurements happened at the end of the experiment, and lack of time prevented more intensive examination.

The following quote from SRI's report* will give you an idea of the actual survey and the results:

*L. T. Dolphin, A. H. Moussa, et al., *Applications of Modern Sensing Techniques to Egyptology* (Menlo Park, California: SRI International, September 1977).

Several anomalies were observed as a result of our resistivity survey at the Sphinx. A very limited number of measurements were taken due to the time scheduling of the project. As a result of the survey, the team discovered five areas of interest.

Behind the rear paws (northwest end) we ran two traverses. Both traverses indicate an anomaly that could possibly be due to a tunnel aligned northwest to southeast.

Another anomaly exists in the middle of the south side near a square cupola added apparently in Roman times. This anomaly was verified by two overlapping traverses. When the electrodes were moved 2 meters away from the previous traverse, the anomaly decreased in value. This is typical of the behavior expected from a vertical shaft.

There are two anomalies in front of the front paws of the Sphinx. The bedrock in front of the Sphinx is covered with Roman-era paving stone and poor electrical contact between the paving stones and bedrock gave somewhat noisy resistivity traverses. However, one anomaly occurs on large electrodes spacings, suggesting a cavity or shaft as much as 10 meters deep. The cavity, if present, is probably filled with rubble.

The bedrock in the area surrounding the Sphinx seems to be competent limestone lacking obvious fissures or veins of mineralized material as observed from the surface. A shallow gully-like area runs southwest to northeast on the south side of the Sphinx approximately one foot wide.

The resistivity anomalies we found around the Sphinx are not defined sufficiently to allow us any absolutely certain conclusions, and we feel that a more detailed survey should be conducted.

The SRI report recommended a much more detailed resistivity survey of the Sphinx to generate 3-D maps of subsurface anomalies. It also suggested use of different techniques to determine anomalies and the use of borescope photography to check those detected before any excavation of an anomaly occurred.

The SRI project was important to the ECF, not only because it found possible hidden cavities near the locations specified by Edgar Cayce, but because it gave the ECF's scholar an opportunity to become acquainted with SRI personnel, and to learn more about the techniques employed. The usefulness of these techniques was proved by the discovery of other anomalies, such as a chamber containing a wooden boat near the Great Pyramid, and anomalies at Thebes, which were not investigated until 1987.

1978: THE SPHINX EXPLORATION PROJECT

The last SRI project suggested exciting possibilities, but provided no final answers. The team discovered numerous anomalies worthy of archaeological exploration around specific structures, both in the Giza plateau and other archaeological spots in Egypt—all without significantly disturbing the existing locales.

During 1977, the ECF's scholar met with the SRI team on his return from his first season with the Nag Hammadi expedition. The preliminary resistivity survey of the Sphinx mentioned in the last project resulted from discussions and suggestions between them. This survey produced encouraging results, and ECF began to fund research at the Sphinx.

ECF and SRI negotiated a contract for an exhaustive remote-sensing survey of the entire Sphinx sanctuary (rock-cut ditch) and the Sphinx Temple, immediately to the east. At the same time SRI performed its survey of the Sphinx for ECF, it conducted a similar program at the first and second Giza pyramids under contract with another party. The fieldwork occurred during the first three months of 1978. The program for the Sphinx project called for a resistivity survey, with data points every square meter over the entire bedrock floor of the Sphinx and its temple; confirmation of anomalies by acoustical sounding; precision drilling of outstanding anomalies; and borescope observation of any cavities. The last step called for direct observation by a borescope camera lowered down the drill hole. Any features they encountered could be observed on a television monitor.

According to SRI's *Interim Report—Sphinx Exploration Project*, the resistivity technique allows detection of voids, provided the depth of the cavity is less than approximately 3 to 5 cavity diameters. It is also sensitive to small cavities near the surface, or to large cavities that are deep. Cavities that are densely packed with rubble could elude detection.

The resistivity survey revealed numerous anomalies, some clearly traceable to faults visible on the surface. Anomalies not obvious from surface indications were studied further by acoustic sounding, and in each case confirmed. But each anomaly, when drilled and inspected by the borescope, proved to be of natural origin.

SRI felt it unlikely that any significant shallow tunnels, tombs, or passages around the Sphinx were missed by this method. Below 4 meters, there is considerably more uncertainty due to (1) the water table, (2) the decreasing sensitivity of the instruments to deep chambers, (3) the possibility of rubble-filled chambers or cavities, and (4) the masking effects of flaws and anomalies.

Unfortunately, not all the anomalies detected at the Sphinx were drilled. A new sounder technique, used only at the end of the project, showed great promise. This method, called "immersion acoustics," basically operated on the same principle as the acoustic sounder, but had a more powerful transmitter that needed to be immersed in water at the bottom of a drilled hole. Through a powerful electric charge, the transmitter sent out sound waves in every direction. The receiver could be placed anywhere within a 20-to 30-meter range; and if it encountered no "hole" or fissure in the rock, a dull thud registered on the receiver. If blocked by a cavity en route, no sound reached the receiver. Operators could determine the size and shape of the cavity by moving the receiver around.

Employing this device, SRI found what it termed "very significant 'shadow zones'" or blind spots, which indicate hidden, subsurface discontinuities, such as cracks, in the bedrock between the transmitter and the receiver. In only three days of work, SRI found several important shadow zones.

Some of these had not appeared on the resistivity surveys. One significant blind spot lies beneath the cupola alongside the Sphinx on the south side. Earlier, SRI had electronically searched for and failed to find a shaft there. The shadow sounder suggests that this area is still suspicious. However, there were no apparent cracks in the surface rock near this blind spot or indications of any filled passages.

The project generated more questions than it answered. Only five of the anomalies were checked with the borescope, and the blind spots remained a mystery; but it became apparent that there was an urgent need for major preservation work on the Sphinx. A thorough cleaning of the Sphinx revealed unknown details, and it was recommended that restoration be started within the next five years in order to save the monument.

The project ended on a note of frustration, because some anomalies had to be left undrilled. Questions remained in the minds of many connected with the project; but the expense of the equipment, contract, and personnel, coupled with numerous internal problems, stopped further investigation.

1978–1982: THE SPHINX MAPPING PROJECT AND STONE DETERIORATION STUDY

Although the Sphinx at Giza is probably the best-known symbol of Egypt and antiquity, by 1979 it had never been meticulously studied and surveyed, nor had large-scale drawings been published. The most extensive excavation of the site, by Baraize from 1925 to 1936, went entirely unpublished. Earlier and subsequent excavations provided only incomplete reports, or none at all. The previous ECF project had shown serious deterioration of the Sphinx and emphasized the scarcity of information about it.

Recognizing the value of a systematic archaeological and architectural survey of the Sphinx, in 1979 archaeologist Mark Lehner presented a proposal to perform such a survey to the American Research Center in Egypt (ARCE). ARCE was originally formed in 1948 to continue Egyptologist George A.

Reisner's work in Giza and Nubia; in 1962, it expanded its aims and purposes and is now a research organization in Egypt based on a consortium of American universities and museums with both public and private funding. ARCE's purpose became "the comprehensive study of all phases of Egyptian and Islamic history and culture from earliest times." It provides a broad range of services attuned to the special needs of individuals and groups working in Egypt.

Mark Lehner's proposal called for work at both the Sphinx and at the small Isis temple located at the foot of the Great Pyramid. Here, in 1858, Auguste Mariette found the "inventory Stela," which states that Khufu, the alleged builder of the Great Pyramid, had found both the Isis temple and the Sphinx in ruined condition and restored them. If one were to believe the text, it would suggest that the Sphinx is much older than conventional Egyptian chronology alleges. Whether the stela Mariette found was a forgery or not, study of the temple offered opportunities to check certain chronological points of the Giza necropolis.

Dr. Paul Walker, then director of ARCE, supported Lehner's proposal. Dr. James Allen, Egyptologist and assistant director of ARCE (Cairo office), agreed to be project director with Mark Lehner as field director. The proposal passed ARCE's review committee and a concession for work was granted by the Egyptian Antiquities Organization (EAO). The ECF was the major financial sponsor of the ARCE Sphinx project, with additional grants from the Chase National Bank of Egypt and the Franzhein Synergy.

Initially, the project consisted of on-site work at the Sphinx, using conventional archaeological tools for survey and study. However, the project soon expanded, becoming international in its participants, and combining conventional surveying techniques with photogrammetry. Photogrammetry is a highly refined technique for producing extremely detailed architectural drawings to scale from carefully surveyed photographs. In September 1979, the German Archaeological Institute in Cairo agreed to donate both personnel and the expensive equipment necessary for a photogrammetric study of the Sphinx, to produce master plans and elevations of the Sphinx showing every structural detail. Later, Dr. K. Lal Gauri, director of the Stone

Conservation Laboratory, department of geology, University of Louisville, Kentucky, joined the project to conduct a diagnosis of the Sphinx and study the means for its preservation. With these additions, the project's purpose broadened.

Two British archaeologists joined the project to work at the Isis Temple in 1980. Dr. Jihan Ragai, an Egyptian chemist at AUC in Cairo, began to analyze samples of ancient stone and mortar. Dr. Christianne Zivie, a French Egyptologist specializing in the Giza necropolis and the New Kingdom, worked with the project for two years.

After three years of cooperation and hard work, from 1979 to 1982, the project accomplished the following: (1) complete architectural documentation of the Sphinx, (2) geological analysis and mapping of the Sphinx site, (3) a diagnosis of deterioration causes on the Sphinx, and (4) preliminary research toward prescribing treatment to preserve the Sphinx. The Sphinx and the entire Sphinx site, which includes three large ancient temples situated in front of the Sphinx, were thoroughly mapped with the same detail. The drawings were made available to the Egyptian Antiquities Organization for its restoration work.

New information emerged as a result of the careful mapping and documentation. In September 1980, a passage was located and recorded in and under the rear part of the Sphinx. Found in 1926 during that full-scale clearing of the Sphinx, it had since been resealed with masonry and cement.

A side benefit of the ARCE Sphinx Survey was the acquisition by ARCE for reproduction and future publication of two hundred archival photos of the 1925–1936 Sphinx excavation. No report has been published on these past excavations since they took place, and the photos are a month-by-month pictorial account of the work.

These photos show that when the Sphinx was first cleared in the 1920s, the excavators took much of the stonework away. They dismantled all the square stonework attachments and dug into the body, probably to look for chambers thought to be concealed by the attached boxes. Two or three photos seem to show a kind of cavity in the north mid-body, with a man standing lower than floor level in the recess. Another shows a definite hole in the south hind paw. These features were all covered up again, with the old stonework and modern cement. This important set of photos has been lying in an institute in Paris all these years.

For the deterioration study, K. Lal Gauri divided the Sphinx rock into four major components for analysis: bedrock, granite, limestone, and mortar. After analysis, he concluded that water-soluble salts were the main cause of deterioration. Such salts would be harmless without water; but a rising water table, moisture from past restoration mortar, and the type of limestone used in repair became major factors in erosion. Interestingly, duricrust, a natural surface coating that prevents erosion and deterioration, appeared on the restoration limestone and mortar prior to 1925–1926; it isn't present on restoration limestone from that date on, because of the type of stone and mortar used.

Various papers and publications resulted from this intensive study and survey, many (such as "Geological Study of the Sphinx" by K. L. Gauri, *ARCE Newsletter*, 1984) focusing on safe restoration guidelines for the Sphinx. The most recent was a paper presented at the 1987 Annual Meeting of the Geological Society of America (October 26 to 29), titled "Evolution of Pore System and Its Influence upon Durability of Limestone at the Great Sphinx."

In 1982, some of the drawings were copyrighted for future publication. To date, however, the original plan to publish a comprehensive atlas on the Sphinx utilizing all this material has yet to be fulfilled. A preliminary report of this survey was published in the *ARCE Newsletter* (1980, no. 112), and it is to be hoped that a complete publication will occur in the near future; it would be a classic in Egyptology.

1982–PRESENT: THE GIZA PLATEAU MAPPING PROJECT

The ARCE Sphinx Mapping Project led to a wider project to map the entire Giza necropolis. Studies of the geology of the Sphinx and its alignment with other monuments on the Giza plateau indicated that the major monuments might be laid out according to a master plan. For example, several unusual discoveries were made during the Sphinx Mapping Project. Egyptologists had previously concluded that the Sphinx Temple was for the worship of the sun. The twenty-four pillars for the colonnades were thought to represent the twenty-four hours of day and night. It seemed perplexing that the axis of the temple does not point at the Sphinx, but passes the Sphinx to the south side of the second Giza pyramid of Khafre. It is just at this point that the sun sets on the equinoxes, when viewed from the eastern sanctuary of the Sphinx Temple. The architectural layout of the temple symbolically divides the day and year in half, and its axis points at the astronomical midyear. On the summer solstice, when the sun has moved as far north as it ever will on the western horizon before starting back south, it sets midway between the two largest Giza pyramids, when viewed from the area of the Sphinx temple.

Could these alignments and configurations have been intentionally planned? Did ancient surveyors lay out the pyramids and establish the relationships of the whole plateau?

These and other alignments connecting the major Giza monuments generated questions and led to the Giza Plateau Mapping Project. Just as a detailed, large-scale map of the Sphinx and its surrounding site had not existed prior to the Sphinx Mapping Project, there was no good large-scale map that included all the ancient architecture plus the topography of the Giza plateau.

Primary funding came from a variety of other sponsors, but ECF also contributed to this worthwhile project. As we have seen, there are clues in the Cayce readings that the structures on the Giza plateau are related.

This project is ongoing, with all ground surveying completed after two seasons of work. A progress report appeared in the *ARCE Newsletter*, no. 131, fall 1985.

The next stage is to use aerial photography to plot the map of the area using photogrammetry. The third stage of the project is to excavate for the ancient harbor and workmen's village in unexplored areas east and south of the pyramids. The initial activities evolving from the Sphinx Mapping Project and the beginning stages of the Giza Plateau Mapping Project resulted in a feature article in the April 1986 *Smithsonian* magazine.

1978–1980: OTHER DISCOVERIES NEAR THE SPHINX

Despite the ambiguous results of the SRI project, a series of fortuitous discoveries by other archaeologists in the late 1970s and early 1980s demonstrated that the area in front of the Sphinx discussed by Cayce is by no means well understood, and the potential exists for many future discoveries.

During the spring of 1978, Zahi Hawass, an Egyptian archaeologist sponsored by the Egyptian Antiquities Organization, began excavations northeast of the Sphinx beside the town of Nazlet el-Samman. Excavation uncovered Roman, New Kingdom, and Middle Kingdom artifacts. April 22 to 24 witnessed a major find: the discovery of an Old Kingdom rock-cut tomb. Robbed in antiquity, it contained the burial pit and statuary of the deceased and his wife carved into the rock of the tomb, as well as some hieroglyphics. This find implies that other important antiquities may lie underneath the town that borders the Sphinx.

In 1980, Egypt's Ministry of Irrigation drilled holes to determine the level of the water table near the digs of Zahi Hawass. The Hawass excavations had found bedrock relatively near the surface. The water drilling was done in September 1980, 15 to 20 meters further east of the Hawass excavations. (Figure 5-3 shows the relation of the drill site to the Sphinx.) It went through 16 meters of soft, unexcavated debris before hitting a solid surface. Thus, between the Hawass site and the drill site, there lies a subsurface dropoff of great depth. From this depth the core drill pulled up a fair-sized chunk of red granite. Red granite is only found naturally in Aswan (400 miles south of Giza), so the granite at this depth must have been culturally introduced by the ancient Egyptians. Both the dropoff and the red granite raise interesting possibilities. The dropoff may be the edge of an ancient harbor, and the granite a chunk that fell off a barge in the Fourth Dynasty. Alterna-

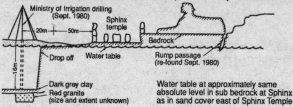

Surface of sand at approximately same absolute level as Sphinx sanctuary bedrock floor

Ministry of Irrigation drilling (Sept. 1980)
Sphinx temple
20m — 50m
Sphinx temple
Bedrock
16m
Drop off   Water table   Rump passage (re-found Sept. 1980)
Dark grey clay
Red granite (size and extent unknown)
Water table at approximately same absolute level in sub bedrock at Sphinx as in sand cover east of Sphinx Temple

Figure 5-3. Map of area in front of Sphinx.

tively, the granite may be a fragment from an ancient temple or monument. If so, the great depth would indicate an origin of extreme antiquity. The questions and possibilities cannot be settled without much more research and excavation.

1982–PRESENT: CARBON DATING THE STRUCTURES ON THE GIZA PLATEAU

The date 10,000 B.C. is central to the Cayce story of Atlantis and Egypt, yet this date is also the aspect of the story considered most unlikely by Egyptologists. The traditional dates for the pyramids, however, are based entirely on historical chronologies, and no technology had ever been employed to arrive at a date objectively. The idea to carbon date the pyramids originated from an A.R.E. tour group in Egypt in November 1982. After discussing archaeological disparities between conventional Egyptology and information given in the Cayce readings, several A.R.E. members expressed an interest in putting the 10,000 B.C. date for the Great Pyramid to the test through Carbon-14 dating, and agreed to financially support the testing through ECF if it could be done. Mark Lehner presented the idea to Dr. Robert J. Wenke, a prehistorian with the University of Washington, who was then also director of ARCE.

Such a study could only have significant value both for radiocarbon dating and Egyptian chronology if the program included a selection of major pyramids from salient points in the Old Kingdom, also known as the Pyramid Age. Ideally, the project planned to obtain five samples from sixteen structures, for a total of eighty samples.

ECF agreed to sponsor the program, at an estimated cost of $17,000. Dr. Wenke located a lab to handle dating—the Radiocarbon Laboratory of the Institute for the Study of Earth and Man at Southern Methodist University, under the supervision of Dr. Herbert Haas. For the smallest samples, where a laboratory with a more sensitive method—accelerator dating—was necessary, Dr. Haas arranged for the Institute of Medium Energy Physics (Eidgenössische Technische Hochschule (ETH Lab)), under the direction of Professor Willy Wölfli in Zurich, Switzerland, to do the carbon dating. A proposal for the sampling and dating program by ARCE, submitted to the Egyptian Antiquities Organization (EAO), was approved, and EAO granted permission for the sampling in December 1983.

Over the three-month period from December 1983 through February 1984, the team collected seventy-one samples from thirteen pyramids, the Sphinx Temple, and a First Dynasty tomb. Several factors caused the original plan to be modified. First, they had great difficulty finding five widely dispersed samples of charcoal or other organic material from each structure to be analyzed, so some structures have a greater number of samples than others. Second, some structures targeted for analysis didn't yield samples conducive to Carbon-14 dating, and some were impossible to obtain due to military restrictions. Finally, gathering, photographing, packaging, and correctly identifying each sample for testing was a long and painstaking task.

Generally, most samples were charcoal from the gypsum mortars. Gypsum mortar appears throughout the exposed surfaces of the Giza pyramids, and charcoal is found here and there in the seams separating the stones. The majority of the Giza samples were obtained from mortar showing between or adhering to the face of core stones where the fine outer casing had been ripped off. In some cases, the charcoal samples were partially showing on the exposed surface of a mortar glob. In other cases, the sample was extracted entirely fresh by cutting the mortar. The team sampled a number of pyramids outside the Giza plateau; but due to difficulties in obtaining good charcoal samples from these other pyramids, more samples were taken instead of the Great Pyramid.

Retrieval of samples from as deep within the core of the Great Pyramid as possible was the ideal. Initially, it was thought these might be obtained from the sides of the forced passages made by early explorers taking off from the interior passages and chambers. There was also the possibility of samples from interior passages and chambers themselves. However, here the joints in the masonry were so fine as to leave no organic inclusions visible to the naked eye, especially in the dim light. Also, the walls of the chambers and passages are partially blackened by torches of those visiting the pyramids before electric lights were installed. It was assumed that samples from here would be too contaminated to be successfully cleaned by the chemical pretreatment applied to all samples in the laboratory.

Another possibility was mortar in the series of five stress-relieving chambers above the King's Chamber. However, it was not possible to obtain permission for the special scaffolding necessary to get these.

In the end, most of the samples came from the outside surface. Sixteen samples, instead of five, were obtained at different levels from the two hundred courses of stones that make up the Great Pyramid:

- 5 samples came from near the base, mostly from masonry course 2
- 4 samples came from course 5
- 1 sample came from course 25
- 1 sample came from course 65
- 1 sample came from courses 108–109
- 3 samples came from course 198
- 1 sample came from the top platform

The final sample was taken from the Grotto, which is dead within the core of the pyramid, close to the center, where massive masonry rests on the original rock floor. A shaft lined with small blocks of limestone is located just past the grotto. This is thought to be either part of the escape route for those who initially closed the pyramid, a forced entrance for ancient robbers, or an air passage for the builders. No organic inclusions were found in the mortar of the blocks lining the shaft. One sample of mortar was taken for microscopic scanning of organic traces, but no carbon compounds were found.

Collecting samples from the Sphinx was also part of the plan. The Sphinx is carved directly out of the natural rock of the Giza plateau, so the carving of the statue cannot be Carbon-14 dated. However, the bottom of the Sphinx is covered with a layered veneer of limestone masonry, and bits of charcoal are in the fill *between* the earliest layers of repair masonry and the natural rock-core body of the Sphinx. The body of the Sphinx was badly weathered before the first layer of masonry was added, so dating the fill would give some idea of the date of the first reconstruction. Unfortunately, due to the official restoration work on the Sphinx during the time of the program, no samples could be obtained from the Sphinx.

The SMU and ETH labs performed painstaking analysis on the samples, and the results were surprising both for the Cayce supporters and the traditional Egyptologists. The dates did not correspond closely to either story!

None of the dates on any of the samples, including those from the Great Pyramid, are close to the 10,000 B.C. time frame found in the Cayce readings. The fourteen dates from the Great Pyramid now in hand from the ETH laboratory in Zurich range from 3100 B.C. to 2850 B.C. These dates include the tree-ring chronology calibration.

Although these preliminary Carbon-14 dates are certainly closer to the Egyptological time frame than that of the Cayce readings, they would still be considered radically early for currently accepted Egyptological chronology. The best way to see this is to examine Figure 5-4, which charts the age differences between the Carbon-14 dates and the historical age.

On February 6, 1986, when the dating had been completed, Herbert Haas commented to the ARE/ECF editorial staff about this chart: "Finally, a histogram of all age dates shows the distribution within a bell-shaped outline, centering at 374 years 'older' than the historic estimate. A scattering of younger ages is present. Many of these are from temples and associated structures, where later intrusive burials are known to occur."

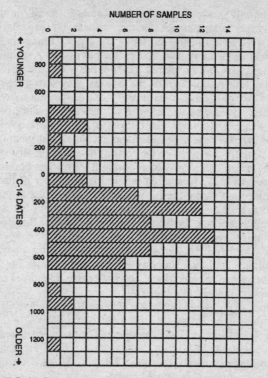

Figure 5-4. Comparison of age differences between Carbon-14 dates and historical age.

Clearly, that was a disappointment to the Edgar Cayce Foundation members who had hoped for verification of Cayce's dates for the Great Pyramid. Just as clearly, these results produced consternation on the part of Egyptologists who viewed them as a "monkey wrench" thrown into their present scheme of historical dating.

The best assessment of the projects is probably that the results are significant enough to raise a lot of questions, and additional investigation is certainly warranted. A more thorough sampling and carbon dating of both the Great Pyramid

Sample & Field No.	LAB	C-14 Age B.C.	Level Sample Retrieved From Pyramid	Difference Between C-14 & Egyptology Dates
10B charcoal	ETH 0312	3809±160	198th level (top platform), sw corner	*1232 years
10B wood	ETH 0334	3101±414	198th level	524 years
06	ETH 0307	3090±153	25-26 level W. side, NW corner	513 years
08	ETH 0309	3062±157	108-109 level, W. side NW corner	485 years
10A	ETH 0311	3020±131	198th level (top platform) SW corner	443 years
14	SMU 1417	2988±319	5th level, S side, SE corner	421 years
14	ETH 0227	2988±170	5th level, S side, SE corner	411 years
13	ETH 0226	2975±168	5th level, SE corner	398 years
04	ETH 0305	2971±120	2nd level; core block N. side off NW corner	384 years
11	ETH 0313	2950±164	Top platform, SW corner, fiber-like charcoal	373 years
15	ETH 0306	2920±100	2nd level, N. side, E. face	352 years
07	ETH 0308	2909±97	65th level W. side, NW corner	332 years
02	ETH 0303	2909±104	2nd level, N. side. E. face	332 years
01	ETH 0302	2869±94	2nd level, N. side, E. end	292 years
13	SMU 1418	2864±362	5th level, SE corner	287 years
03	ETH 0304	2853±104	2nd level, N. face, off NW corner	276 years

* This date was on a miniscule fraction of black material which was not identified. The date has not been included in the analyses of the results.

2nd and 5th level mean of 9 dates   2928±69
25th,65th & 108th levels. mean of 3 dates   3020±80
198th top levels, mean of 3 dates   3024±154

Mean of all 15 dates   2986±52

Figure 5-5. Calibrated dates of the Great Pyramid at Giza.

and other Egyptian monuments might well turn up more details and more puzzling data when compared to the present accepted time frame of Egyptian chronologies.

One other interesting result from this project is the data in Figure 5-5. When we compare the dates of samples taken from the top levels of the Giza pyramid to the dates of those taken from the bottom, the dates of the top layers tend to be older than those from the lower level of the pyramid! Although there is a range of uncertainty in the dates, it appears that the top of the pyramid is at least two hundred years older than the bottom. The pyramid could not have been built from the top down, so this discrepancy may mean repairs were made on the bottom layers at a later time. Another possible explanation is the burning of progressively older wood scraps during the preparation of the mortar for the upper portions of the pyramid. Unfortunately, no samples were taken from the core of the pyramid or from the Sphinx during this project.

The results of this carbon dating project have not yet been published, but they have been presented twice to the scientific community. The first presentation was in November/December 1986 at the International Colloquium by the Centre National de Recherche Scientifique (CNRS), at the University of Lyon in France, on "Relative Chronologies and Absolute Chronology for the Near East." Herbert Haas presented a report on these findings, which has been published with the colloquium's other presentations by the *British Archaeological Record* in the International Series, Vol. 379 (ii), pp. 585–606. The second presentation, which we will discuss later, was given by Dr. Haas in Cairo, Egypt, at another international conference.

1987: "TECHNOLOGY OPENS ANCIENT DOORS"

On February 24, 1987, the *New York Times* ran this headline for an article on archaeological discoveries made using modern remote-sensing technology in Egypt during January 1987. An undiscovered tomb was detected by magnetometer in the

Valley of the Kings, located in Thebes, on the west side of the Nile from Karnak and Luxor. This discovery resulted from the Berkeley Theban Mapping Project of the entire Theban complex. (Interestingly, in 1976, SRI found an area it had thought worthy of investigation ten years earlier, and had recommended future work in the same spot.) At the end of the article, the *New York Times* quoted Zahi Hawass, now chief inspector of the Giza Pyramids, as saying that French and Japanese research teams, using seismic and magnetic remote sensing, had recently detected several hollows in the Great Pyramid and under the Sphinx.

Apparently, the introduction of high-tech modalities into archaeology, which SRI had initiated ten years earlier and in which ECF became involved in 1977, has been refined and accepted and is now being used much more widely. It offers exciting prospects for future archaeological investigation. Much research remains to determine if anything of archaeological value may be uncovered in these detected "suspicious" zones in both the Giza plateau and other archaeological sites in Egypt.

The story of the search in Egypt has been one of slow progress over many years; but 1987 saw an explosion of new finds, as the new technology began to be applied in earnest. The Japanese and French discoveries, coupled with some of the efforts described here, led to an exciting conference in Cairo, Egypt, from December 14 to 17, 1987, entitled, "The First International Symposium on the Application of Modern Technology to Archaeological Explorations at the Giza Necropolis." It was attended by leading scientists from around the world. At this conference, Herbert Haas presented for the second time to the scientific community the findings from the ECF-sponsored radiocarbon-dating project, and offered convincing evidence that Egyptian chronology needs to be reconsidered. The following excerpts from his report at this symposium jolt the accepted Egyptian chronology:

All radiocarbon dates on samples of unquestionable origin and quality are older than their historical record.

The largest number of samples, fifteen, were taken from the Khufu pyramid, whose average calibrated ra-

diocarbon age is 2966 ± 50 years B.C. This is approximately 390 years older than the midpoint of Khufu's
reign according to the tabulation of Cambridge Ancient
History.

Sources of error of the radiocarbon method, like use
of old wood or undetected contamination, are not likely
to produce the observed pattern of age differences.

Although Cayce's dates for the building of the Great Pyramid
don't coincide with these, neither do those of the Egyptologists. Again, much more research is necessary to discover how
old these structures really are.

The presentations at this symposium on the Sphinx and the
Great Pyramid, by a team led by Sakuji Yoshimura from Wa-
seda University in Japan, were also exciting from the Cayce
perspective. The Japanese used two types of ground-
penetrating radar. One measured reflections from underground
objects, and the other looked for cavities by measuring radar
transmission through rock. They found a number of cavities
in the Great Pyramid, confirming and extending the findings
of a team of French researchers in 1986. Some cavities contain
sand; but there appears to be a 30-meter-long passage that
starts behind the west side of the north wall of the "Queen's
Chamber." Near the Great Pyramid, the Japanese scanned the
famous boat pits. One had been opened years ago, and contained a wooden funeral boat from the time of Khufu. The
other has not been opened, but a group sponsored by the National Geographic Society drilled into it, sampled the air, and
photographed a disassembled boat.

Near the Sphinx, the Japanese discovered underground cavities, which go beyond the findings of the SRI projects ten
years before and offer the possibility that Cayce's "Hall of
Records" may yet be found. Near the right paw, they found
a possible tunnel 2.5 to 3 meters below the ground surface.
Other measurements suggested the possibility of a tunnel under the Sphinx. They found several other cavities, which they
felt might contain metal or granite. At this time, there is no
way to know what these cavities and tunnels may be. One
possibility, brought up by Herbert Haas, is that they may be
small natural cavities filled with iron-rich compounds depos-

ited by groundwater flow. The Japanese plan further investigation, including drilling, to answer the question with solid evidence.

What have been the results of the Edgar Cayce Foundation's efforts in Egypt? It is true that no records of Atlantis have been uncovered, and that the age of the Sphinx and the Great Pyramid is still unknown. What has been shown is the need for further investigation. Many mysteries remain, even after two hundred years of archaeological exploration in Egypt.

Although Egyptologists do not dispute the assertion that people have lived for thousands of years in the Nile valley, they consider any life prior to 4000 B.C. to have been that of a Stone Age culture. Generally, Egyptologists believe the civilization that built the pyramids and other monuments began around 4000 B.C. About 3150 B.C., forces from the south of Egypt conquered the north and united the country under the First Dynasty of Menes. The pyramids at Giza came later, about 2700 B.C., and the Great Pyramid at Giza is assigned to Cheops or Khufu of the Fourth Dynasty. Evidence cited for this chronology is the Greek historian Herodotus, who records that Khufu was the builder of the Great Pyramid. Even more persuasive is the presence of graffiti giving Khufu's name in sealed chambers of the pyramid that were not opened until modern times.

Arrayed against this evidence is the Cayce data, but this data does not stand alone. Ancient Arab historians say Hermes, with Ra, built the Great Pyramid. The *Book of the Dead*, an old Egyptian text, as well as ancient legends, speak of underground chambers near the Sphinx. The Egyptian historian Manetho pushes Egyptian culture back 13,000 years. Slate palettes, with carvings indicating a level of culture well above Stone Age, have been discovered in sites over 5,000 years old. An inventory stela was found that tells of Khufu's finding the Temple of Isis in ruins and of making repairs to the Sphinx. Scars matching the description can still be seen.

One of the most puzzling questions regarding the Great Pyramid is how it was built. It is estimated that the Great Pyramid is composed of over 2 million blocks, some weighing over 13 tons. To even put this many blocks in place, much less to quarry and move them, would require placing a block every five minutes, twenty-four hours a day for twenty years. This does not even include the time necessary to design such a structure or allow for adverse weather conditions during building. To build a pyramid in this short a time would obviously be an impossible task, even with modern equipment.

These and other puzzles still defy explanation. As for the specific work of the ECF, even though some of the anomalies discovered in the SRI survey of the Sphinx proved to be of natural origin, not all were drilled. What of the openings in the Sphinx that were cemented up, shown in the photos of the 1925 expedition? The results of the Japanese investigation suggest that there is much to be discovered. For the Great Pyramid, carbon dates determined from the few samples taken did not agree with Cayce's dates, but they did not agree with accepted dates either. Obviously, more sampling is called for. The most exhaustive study and mapping of the Sphinx remains to be published. Unfortunately, many of Egypt's mysteries remain mysteries awaiting future explorations.

1988 TO ?: FUTURE RESEARCH AND POSSIBLE DISCOVERIES

The Edgar Cayce Foundation, dedicated individuals, and other organizations are still intensely interested in unraveling these mysteries and are proceeding as funds permit:

- The eventual publication of the *Atlas of the Sphinx* by Robert Wenke, Mark Lehner, James Allen, and others.
- The Giza Mapping Project—an ongoing effort by ARCE and Mark Lehner, Zahi Hawass, and others. As mentioned, only the first step of this project is completed, and the next two steps offer possibilities for discoveries similar to or as significant as those described in the *New York Times* that resulted from the Theban Mapping Project.
- An entirely new project, independent of the Edgar Cayce Foundation, is presently being launched by Renée Kra, the managing editor of *Radiocarbon*, a journal devoted to radiocarbon dating that is published at Yale University.

The last project, titled the "International Radiocarbon Data Base" (IRDB), will establish a centrally located computerized data base with universal sanctions from an international community of radiocarbon dates and consumers of dates (namely, archaeologists). All radiocarbon dates will be stored on a mainframe computer, continually updated, and instantly accessible to researchers worldwide through telecommunications. The third planning conference was held at Yale University in March 1988. The initial pilot project will probably utilize radiocarbon data obtained from ancient Egypt.

Let us now turn west to the Bahamas and see if discoveries off the coast of Florida have turned up any clues pertaining to Atlantis.

6

THE SEARCH FOR ATLANTIS IN BIMINI

YES, WE HAVE the land known as Bimini, in the Atlantic Ocean . . . this is the highest portion left above the waves of a once great continent, upon which the civilization as now exists in the world's history found much of that as would be used as means for attaining that civilization'' (no. 996–1, August 14, 1926).

Cayce gave his first reading on Bimini, not for archaeologists eager to find evidence of Atlantis, but for a group of businessmen—treasure hunters who wanted to get rich quick. The Bimini readings were part of a large set of readings given in a search for treasure and oil in Florida and Bimini. Despite months of effort, they found no treasure, and oil proved elusive as well. The readings explained, ''. . . information as is given through the manifestation of the Universal Forces as are manifested through this body, Edgar Cayce, in the subconscious or unconscious forces, is for the up-lifting, and should never be used for other than that . . .'' (no. 996–10, February 24, 1927).

As an appropriately uplifting project, the readings suggested development of an archaeological and healing resort, and gave detailed plans for financing and constructing such a project. The plans included instructions for drilling a well to obtain fresh water, and directions for finding healing sulfur water and minerals to help finance the project. Although plans for a resort have not yet come to fruition, the readings sparked a search for Atlantis that continues to this day, with increasing controversy.

Why is the idea of a sunken civilization in Bimini so controversial? The situation in Bimini contrasts with that in Egypt. In Egypt, it is easy to find ruins; the problem is proving their age or that they have anything to do with Atlantis. In Bimini, the problem is to find anything at all. If any remains of a high civilization were to be found, even the strongest skeptics would have to consider the possibility of Atlantis. We saw earlier that geologists accept that the Bahama Bank was above water at the time Cayce gave for Atlantis, and was submerged by the rising sea level with the melting of the glaciers. But the remains of ancient people found submerged in similar areas are of primitive Stone Age culture, not the cities and temples of Cayce's Atlantis. Archaeologists did not take the Cayce readings seriously in his day, because the Bahama bank had been underwater at least 8,000 years, and they felt that human beings probably had not even been in North America that long. More recently, despite new evidence, claims of submerged cities still do not fit the current archaeological concept of ancient human occupation of America. With so little to go on from the readings, much less than in Egypt, exploration of the area has progressed slowly.

THE EARLY EXPLORATIONS

After their initial hunt for treasure, the people who requested the original readings from Cayce appear to have abandoned their quest. Despite the advice given in the readings in the 1920s, no one actually tried to build a resort on the island.

The search was revived in 1935, when a woman who was one of the first female airplane pilots became intrigued by the readings, and flew to Bimini in search of a well. It is not clear what the inspiration for her search was. The freshwater well mentioned in reading no. 996–12 required drilling down to 892 feet, while the sulfur water was said to be at a depth of 90 feet. Gladys Davis, Edgar Cayce's stenographer, thought perhaps the idea had arisen during conversations with Cayce about things he saw on his trip to Bimini with the treasure hunters in 1927.

Whatever her source of information, the pilot flew to Bimini, and reported finding "a fresh-water well . . . walled around the top with stones of peculiar composition and strange symbols," according to correspondence files at the Edgar Cayce Foundation. In reading no. 587–4, she asked Cayce to comment on this discovery. He responded much the same way he had to the treasure hunters:

> For it could be established as a center for two particular purposes; a regeneration for those with certain types of individual ailments (not only from the well, or water from same, but from surrounding waters—because of the life in same), and a center for archaeological research. And as such activities are *begun*, there will be found much more gold in the lands under the sea than there is in the world circulation today!
>
> . . . But this should *not* be left alone; it should be considered from many angles.
>
> Also, aid may be induced from the varied societies that have been formed for the study of geological and archaeological activities, or such. For much will be found.
>
> And, as may be known, when the changes begin, these portions will rise among the first. (no. 587–4, July 1, 1935)
>
> [Another reading gave some more information:] . . . In the sunken portions of Atlantis, or Poseidia, where a portion of the temples may yet be discovered, under the slime of ages of seawater—near what is known as Bimini, off the coast of Florida. (no. 440–5, December 20, 1933)

Once again, no one followed the advice of the readings, and the question of Atlantis in Bimini was to lie dormant for many years. Various people familiar with the readings undoubtedly made explorations during the 1940s and 1950s; but if they found anything, no record remains. The archives of the Edgar Cayce Foundation tell of one expedition, however, whose story illustrates the potential and the problems with the search for Atlantis.

Joe Gouveia, a pilot and Cayce enthusiast, organized the expedition in 1957, and involved amateur archaeologists and businessmen interested in the Cayce readings. This group was excited by reports of underwater columns, conceivably the remains of the temple spoken of by Cayce. Plagued by occasional rough weather and with no way to navigate to sites accurately, they had little opportunity to search. They found columns and granite blocks, but had no way of confirming whether these artifacts were the remains of an Atlantean temple, or had fallen from a recent shipwreck.

One puzzling discovery from this expedition remains unexplained, but published photographs suggest something far more unusual than ship's ballast. In 1957, Dr. William Bell, an expedition member from North Carolina, was diving in 40 feet of water when he noticed a vertical column rising several feet from the seabed. It was about 4 inches in diameter at the top, 8 to 10 inches at the bottom, and penetrated the mud of the seabed. Just beneath the bottom mud was a gear-like shape on the column, about two feet in diameter. Lying around the column were a large number of stone slabs. The most unusual part of Bell's discovery is the photographic record. He took several pictures, which showed fogging patterns around the column. In *The Stones of Atlantis*, explorer David Zink published these pictures, and discussed the possibility that radiation from the columns had fogged the film. There is no way to know whether some kind of radiation was responsible, or whether there was simply an error in developing. Bell took cross-bearings on Bimini landmarks, but in the 1970s Zink was unable to relocate the column. Its true nature is likely to remain a mystery, but it served to encourage future explorers to continue the search for the elusive Atlantis.

A GEOLOGIST EXPLORES BIMINI

In 1940, as a brief aside in a reading, Cayce said, "And Poseidia will be among the first portions of Atlantis to rise again. Expect it in sixty-eight or sixty-nine [1968 or 1969]; not so far away!" (no. 958–3).

As the prophesied rise in "sixty-eight or sixty-nine" drew near, the search for Atlantis intensified. For the first time, it involved a professional geologist. He could see that the potential controversy might hurt his professional reputation, so he chose to remain anonymous, and simply called himself "the geologist." His book, *Earth Changes*, first published in 1959, was the first attempt to give serious scientific consideration to the Cayce material. In the 1960s, he turned his attention to Bimini.

The geologist wanted to pursue the Cayce concept of an archaeological and healing resort, neglected since the 1930s. He developed a plan for a resort based on the readings, and proceeded to search for the minerals and fresh water Cayce had said would be found on the islands:

. . . for these mountain tops [the Bimini Islands]—especially that along the north and eastern shores of the north and northern portion of the south island—will produce many various minerals and various other conditions that will be remunerative when the projects are undertaken. (no. 996–12, March 2, 1927)

[Q-1.] Is this the continent known as Alta or Poseidia [Atlantis]?

[A-1.] A temple of the Poseidians was in a portion of this land.

[Q-2.] What minerals will be found here?

[A-2.] Gold, spar, and icthyolite [?].

[Q-3.] How deep in the ground will that be found?

[A-3.] In the wall that would be builded from the western portion of the south island towards that of the *prominent* portions of the southern portions of the isle—these will be found in the 12 to 15 foot levels. The *vein*, as workable, would be found extending in the northeast southwest direction. . . . (no. 996–12, March 2, 1927)

[The call for geological exploration of Bimini was also given in a later reading.] The British West Indies or Bahamas, and a portion of same that may be seen in the present—if the geological survey would be made in some of these—especially, or notably, in Bimini and in the Gulf Stream through this vicinity these may be even yet determined. (no. 364-3, February 16, 1932).

The geologist reviewed the existing information on the geology of Bimini, and concluded that the statements in the readings were reasonable. Although the coral and carbonate rocks found in much of the area do not normally contain minerals, if the Bimini islands were the remains of mountaintops, minerals might be found.

The geologist carried his search to Bimini itself, and in 1965 drilled cores to look for the mineral deposits. He was encouraged in his quest by findings of unusual types of rock during channel dredging in the area. Unfortunately, all he found in the cores he drilled were the usual carbonate rocks of the Bahamas, and no veins of minerals. In 1967, he returned and found gray and brown slate, but still no minerals. He considered his drilling inconclusive, because some of the holes didn't penetrate all the way down to 12 or 15 feet, as specified by the readings.

1968—YEAR OF DISCOVERY?

In 1968, the year predicted by Cayce for the rise of Atlantis, a dramatic event occurred. Two pilots, Trigg Adams and Robert Brush, spotted what appeared to be the underwater foundation of a building near Andros Island, the closest large island to Bimini. Shortly thereafter, a zoologist and amateur archaeologist named J. Manson Valentine, along with Dmitri Rebikoff, a noted underwater explorer and photographer, found what appeared to be the remains of a wall or road about one-half mile off Bimini. According to Robert Marx in *Argosy* of November 1971, the race for Atlantis began in earnest.

The "road" site, which was easily accessible by small boat, received most of the attention. It consisted of huge stone blocks, lined up in what appeared to be a pavement stretching for hundreds of feet across the ocean bottom in about 15 feet of water. In some sections of the site, the blocks were almost perfectly rectangular, and looked very much manmade. In

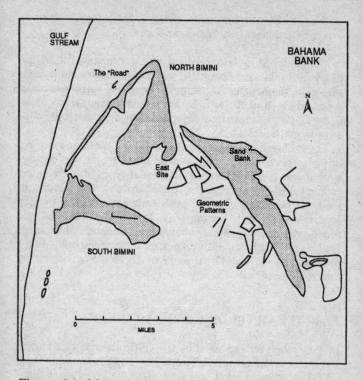

Figure 6-1. Map of Bimini area, showing archaeological sites.

other parts of the site, the blocks seemed to be more randomly arranged. At one end of the site, the pavement made a 90-degree turn, making the site look like a huge reversed J.

Valentine and Rebikoff joined forces with Adams and Brush to form the Marine Archaeology Research Society (MARS), and tried to obtain permits from the Bahamas government to excavate the sites. Meanwhile, the owners of the land on shore nearest the "road" site obtained exclusive rights for themselves. They allowed some geologists and archaeologists to study the road site, but excluded the MARS group and the many amateurs who flocked to see the discoveries. People were allowed to dive on the site, but not to disturb it. *Atlantis: The Autobiography of a Search*, by Robert Ferro and Michael Grumley, chronicles the efforts of some of these amateurs. Prohibiting site excavation was good archaeological practice, but frustrating to those who wanted to find out quickly whether the Cayce readings were right. The newspapers were full of unsubstantiated stories of Atlantean "temples," but few facts. The Cayce readings were frequently misquoted. He did *not* say that a *temple* would be discovered in 1968 or 1969; he said that portions of Atlantis would *rise*. His mention of a temple was in an entirely different reading (no. 440–5), and no discovery date was given.

Two groups in the early 1970s were given permission to conduct more intensive study of the road site. One was led by a geologist named Wyman Harrison. In contrast to the large number of popular magazine and newspaper articles claiming that the site was Atlantis, Harrison published a skeptical article in a 1971 *Nature* in which he gave alternative natural explanations for the origin of the site. He felt that the giant blocks were simply natural beachrock. Beachrock, common in the Bahamas, is a rock formed in slabs along beaches. It tends to fracture, and the fractured pieces often resemble large blocks. Harrison pointed out that the site was approximately parallel to the beach, and that it seemed to consist of a single layer of blocks lying on the bottom. Despite its unusual appearance, he felt it was just a natural geological formation. Harrison also discussed the sunken columns found by earlier explorers, and suggested that they might have come from a shipwreck, since they did not seem to be arranged like any type of building.

The other group was led by John Gifford, a geology student working on his master's thesis at the University of Miami. He did a thorough study of the geology of the area, and came to much the same conclusion as Harrison: that the blocks were a natural formation. But Gifford's interest in the area persisted, and he joined forces with two amateur archaeologists, Talbot Lindstrom and Steven Proctor, founders of the Scientific Exploration and Archaeology Society (SEAS). SEAS expeditions continued to study the area during the 1970s, in the hope of finding other sites that would provide better evidence. One of their most interesting discoveries was a site they named "Proctor's Road," after the discoverer. This new site, near the famous road, was very different. It consisted of clumps of stones, at regular intervals, running in a straight line for over a mile across the bottom. It ran diagonally across old beach lines, and was not parallel to shore, so beachrock was an unlikely explanation. But what function could a manmade structure of this type serve? It didn't lead to anything obviously ancient. At one end was a shipwreck; but the explorers found large metal tanks that proved that the shipwreck was of recent age, and not related to the stones. Lindstrom wrote up the discoveries in articles in the March 1982 *Explorer's Journal* and the *Epigraphic Society Occasional Publications* of 1980, but most archaeologists paid little attention.

The great cost of underwater archaeology, and the difficulties in obtaining excavation permits, limited the amount of serious work that could be done near Bimini. Most of the visitors were simply tourists, trying a day of diving at the site, but not seriously studying it. The initial excitement faded until it was reawakened in 1974, when a new explorer, Dr. David Zink, appeared on the scene.

THE ZINK EXPEDITIONS

Zink began a series of expeditions that were to provide the most intensive study of the Bimini road site of any researcher; yet they still failed to convince most scientists that it was truly the remains of Atlantis. His book, *The Stones of Atlantis*, provides the best information we have on the road site, but his speculations have caused skeptics to question his work.

David Zink was a professor of English at Lamar University in Texas. He had a long-term interest in psychics, Atlantis, and the Cayce readings. Not an archaeologist by training, he felt none of the "anomaly anxiety" of the mainstream archaeologists and geologists like Harrison who were dismissing Bimini. He brought with him the expertise of a generalist: blue-water sailing experience, scuba diving, underwater photography, and a career as a military communications officer and former professor at the Air Force Academy. His library research on Atlantis, and reports of the Bimini discoveries, convinced him to take leave from his university and to continue the search in person. He would eventually resign from the academic world altogether to devote all his time to the search for Atlantis.

In the winter of 1974, Zink and his wife and children sailed their 35-foot sloop 800 miles across the Gulf of Mexico and around the tip of Florida to Bimini. In Miami, he met with J. Manson Valentine, who shared with him the details of the new discoveries and led him to choose the road site as his primary site.

Others, like Rebikoff and Gifford, had studied small sections of the site in detail; but Zink was the first to survey the entire site and attempt to decipher its structure. The overall site has the form of a huge reversed letter J. Its long arm, about 1,900 feet in length, is composed of two parallel rows of large blocks that run not quite parallel to the beach, about one-half mile from shore, and terminate against a wide pavement-like section of smaller, less organized blocks. The pavement section turns through a 90-degree arc toward the beach. Several more parallel sections of stone blocks make up the other arm of the J. In his five weeks at the site, Zink was sufficiently impressed by the regularity of the huge stones to begin plans for a much larger expedition the following year.

Zink's "Poseidia '75" expedition reignited the controversy about the road site. With two boats and the loan of the onshore flat of author Peter Tompkins, Zink assembled a group of over a dozen divers, archaeologists, and geologists to carry out detailed mapping of the blocks in the site. Whereas others had made generalizations based on the few very regular blocks in the short arm of the J, Zink found unusual stones throughout the site. These stones convinced him that the site was not a road, but perhaps a megalithic site similar to Stonehenge.

He assembled several lines of evidence that suggested that the site had been constructed by human beings. First was the site's overall pattern. The parallel rows of blocks were approximately parallel to the current beachline, and could be the remains of ancient beachlines; but the curved pavement was hard to explain except as human handiwork. Certain individual stones also did not fit the standard description of beachrock. Some were resting on smaller stones, like the dolmens of the megalithic sites of Europe, rather than directly on the bottom. Others had distinct geometrical shapes—for example, square, wedge shaped, and arrow shaped. Could these be the result of random fracturing of beachrock? There is also a place where a fracture in the sea bottom runs under the blocks in a different orientation from the block fractures themselves. Finally, measurements of the site suggested numerical patterns and angles to Zink.

The most exciting discoveries that summer were what appeared to be a 300-pound stylized marble "head" sculpture, and a tongue-in-groove building block, both lying on the bottom near the road site. Prior to these discoveries, no one had seen any artifacts other than the stone blocks. If these were proved to be only beachrock, there was nothing left to connect the site with Atlantis. The marble block was clearly not native to the Bahamas. Unfortunately, it was also undatable, and not even clearly a sculpture. Since it and the building block had been found lying on the sea bottom, skeptics felt that they could simply have fallen off a ship. The head remained on the bottom, because Zink had neither the equipment nor the permit required to raise it.

During the winter of 1976, Zink prepared to raise the head the following summer. Word of his discoveries spread, and the International Explorers Society of Florida named him Explorer of the Year. In the summer of 1976, he was contacted by the Cousteau Society, and guided Philippe Cousteau around the Bimini sites in the film "*Calypso*'s Search for Atlantis."

In Zink's primary expedition of that year, Poseidia '76, one of the authors of this book (Douglas Richards) was a member. It was a more focused expedition than the earlier ones; its objectives were to refine the survey of the site and raise the marble head. The site survey was easily accomplished. Using a theodolite on the beach, we measured angles to buoys placed at key points on the site, and constructed the first accurate chart of the site. Earlier maps, such as those of Valentine, were found to be off by as much as a mile, a constant problem with charts in this area. Using solar sightings, we confirmed that magnetic anomalies tend to throw off magnetic compass surveys. The attempt to recover the head did not fare as well. Tropical storm Dottie blew up 12-foot waves, and the head could not be found.

Finally, in 1977, the head was raised from the bottom. Zink was also able to obtain equipment for professional coring of the stone blocks, although the results of his coring were inconclusive.

Zink's work was highly publicized, but the presentation in his book made it unlikely that most archaeologists would take the work seriously. Simply concluding that the site was Atlantean would have been enough to annoy many archaeologists; but Zink went further. Based on readings from psychics on the site, he concluded that extraterrestrials from the Pleiades had been involved in the site's construction.

These claims did not go unchallenged. Eugene Shinn, a geologist with the U.S. Geological Survey (USGS), conducted a study to determine whether the blocks were manmade or of natural origin. Although he was an orthodox geologist, he noted in his article in a 1980 *Nature*, coauthored with archaeologist Marshall McKusick, that the study was at his own expense and not part of a USGS-sponsored project. That even a skeptical article has a disclaimer like this points up the controversial nature of the subject.

Shinn did not look at Zink's claims of the site's unusual structure. Instead of arguing over the overall pattern of the site, he focused on the internal structure of the blocks to tell whether they had been fractured naturally in place or whether people had arranged them. He reasoned that blocks that had formed in place and fractured would have identical sediment layers in adjacent blocks. Blocks that had been moved by human agency would be likely to show different patterns. Shinn drilled cores into adjacent blocks, carefully noting the orientation of the cores. X-ray photographs of some of the cores showed similar bedding planes and angles, convincing Shinn that the blocks had been formed as beachrock on a sloping beach and fractured in place. But not all of his cores gave such clean results. Cores from the north part of the site had large pebbles, which prevented bed formation. Shinn still concluded that these blocks were naturally fractured beachrock, but there were certainly differences in different parts of the site.

Shinn also tried to date the blocks using the Carbon-14 method. The spread of dates was quite wide, but ranged around 3,000 years ago. This was far too recent for the Cayce Atlantis. Unfortunately, it also didn't agree with various other estimates of the age of the site. Sea-level curves from other locations indicate that the site should have been long under water by 3,000 years ago, so it couldn't have formed on a beach. In their *Nature* article, McKusick and Shinn explain away the discrepancy by saying that a substantial amount of sand eroded from underneath the blocks, submerging them to their present depth. The issue is more complicated, however. Zink discusses dates obtained in John Gifford's search, and compares them with ancient sea-level curves. The dates range from 6,000 years ago to 2,500 years ago, with the underlying bedrock dating to 15,000 years ago. With this wide spread of dates, it is hard to draw any conclusion at all about the site. Zink acknowledged the problem, and this part of his discussion was as skeptical as the McKusick and Shinn article.

What was the end result of the Zink expeditions? First, he set a precedent of thorough study of the site. None of his critics has ever looked at the site as thoroughly. Although he is not a professional archaeologist, he understood the importance of mapping, rather than looting, a site. His plans, which show the positions of the individual stones in the road site, will have lasting value. Unfortunately, his work largely served to confirm to many geologists and archaeologists that the site is of natural origin—ancient beachrock, fractured naturally in place with no human intervention. The anomalies of the site, such as the 90-degree bend and the large stones on top of smaller stones, have been seen as insignificant in comparison to the general impression that the site closely resembles natural beachrock forming on the adjacent shoreline. The evidence is certainly not all in, and is still open to interpretation: but it is clear that it will be difficult to prove that the road site in isolation is the ruins of Atlantis.

The road is not the only archaeological site in the area. What of the other sites studied by Zink? Do they offer greater possibilities of proof?

Valentine discovered an unusual bottom pattern immediately to the east of North Bimini, which Zink called the East

Site. Something beneath the sand causes the seagrass to form sharply defined geometrical patterns. Zink did not have the resources to excavate it, but realized that there might be something unusual here. In finding other sites, he was not so lucky. Despite an extensive search, he was unable to relocate the column found by Bell in the 1950s. His expeditions in 1978, 1979, and 1980 found some unusual geological phenomena, such as an apparent underwater hot spring, but no new ruins.

Zink did succeed in eliminating some other sites from consideration, a useful service to future explorers. On a trip to the Andros "temple" site, championed by Valentine, Zink discovered that the walls were not made of worked stone, but crude piles of rocks. He thought it likely that the walls had been built as a sponge pen by fishermen. Zink also demonstrated that a wreck some had thought to be Phoenician was in fact from the 1880s. He checked out stories of granite blocks on the Moselle Shoal north of Bimini, but found modern quarry marks, laying to rest the speculations that this non-native stone had been left by Atlanteans. Zink dropped from the Bimini scene in 1980, leaving many questions about the sites but few answers.

Zink's work certainly did have some problems. Despite his extensive survey work, his presentation was not up to archaeological standards, and criticism was inevitable. But McKusick and Shinn, and later McKusick himself in *Archaeology* of 1984, went far beyond criticisms of unorthodox research. They devote much of their article to an attack on the Cayce "religious cult," interpreting the Bimini controversy as a "clash between scientific interpretation and religious dogma." As readers of this book have seen, nothing could be further from the truth. The Cayce readings are an unorthodox source of information, to be sure, but there is nothing inherently anti-science about them. The purpose of this book has been to show the scientific parallels with the Cayce readings, many of which will undoubtedly surprise most archaeologists. But there are definitely some problem areas in the Cayce readings, as we have shown in previous chapters. Bimini looked like one of the best chances to prove or disprove concepts in the Cayce material, yet years of work have failed to resolve the controversy. Is there any hope of finding other sites on which it might be easier to get scientific agreement?

THE EXPLORERS OF THE 1980S AND BEYOND

The work of the 1960s and 1970s showed that a great deal of effort can be put into this type of project, with little substantial result to show for it. It was like the man who searches for his lost car keys under the lamppost; he doesn't think that's where he lost them, but it's where the light is! The road site occupied so much of everyone's time, skeptic and believer alike, because it was so easy to find. The many other sites reported, some with impressive photographs of grid patterns and circles, were never there again when the time came to explore them, or they were too far away from land to explore. The navigation charts for that area were so poor that even figuring out where you were accurately enough to return was often an insurmountable obstacle. The cost of making good charts was far beyond the resources of those largely amateur undertakings.

Meanwhile, however, technology was developing tools that would change the whole course of exploration. Primary among these high-technology tools were satellite photography, satellite navigation, and side-scan sonar. Together, they would allow precise mapping of the shallow banks and the deep ocean. For the first time, it would be possible to take Cayce's advice literally: "If a geological survey would be made in some of these, especially, or notably in Bimini and in the Gulf Stream through this vicinity, these may even yet be determined" (no. 364–3, February 16, 1932).

The first satellite photograph of the Bimini area was taken in 1973 by the *Landsat 1* satellite, but it was not until ten years later that anyone looked at it in search of archaeological sites. It covered a wide area, thousands of square miles, but the smallest object it could resolve had to be over 200 feet wide. This is good for producing large-scale charts, but not for finding archaeological sites. Nevertheless, unusual geometric patterns showed clearly in the satellite photo, including pentagons and rectangles. In 1984, the first *Landsat 4* photo became available, using much improved technology. In it the geometric patterns were even more clearly visible, and an expedition was planned to find out what they were.

The expedition in 1984 was small compared to the years of work by others, but its purpose was to address a very important question: could photography from satellites be used to locate sites and navigate to them? Navigation had been the perennial problem in looking for the ruins of Atlantis. There are countless stories of discoveries, such as Bell's mysterious column, which were never relocated. Bimini is a small, very flat island, and the only landmark is a tall radio tower on South Bimini. From a few miles away, even this tower is usually invisible in the haze. For this reason, early explorers stayed close to shore. The famous road site was only one-half mile off the shore of North Bimini, and even then it could take several hours for people to find if they didn't know exactly where to look. Yet there remain hundreds of square miles near Bimini to be explored.

The satellite photos showed unusual bottom patterns for many miles around Bimini, but there was no guarantee that they could be found from the surface. Our 1984 expedition went to Bimini armed with satellite photos and maps made from the photos, to locate the patterns in person. The expedition included one of the authors of this book (Douglas Richards), Marty Obando, who is a boat captain and amateur archaeologist, and several people from the Edgar Cayce Foundation.

Our first goal was to find the patterns from the air, using the photos as navigation charts. We chartered a four-seater plane and pilot from Miami. The plane was a high-wing Cessna so that we could open the windows, lean out, and take unobstructed pictures. Quite a thrill at 7,000 feet up! The weather was perfect with a few clouds, but none obstructed the view. The bottom patterns looked just like those in the satellite photo. We crisscrossed the area, taking picture after picture of geometric formations, looking for small details that might confirm whether they were natural or manmade. It was easy to see why some of the patterns had never been discovered. They are so large that only from a satellite can you appreciate their regularity. Some revealed interesting internal details from low altitudes. The mile-wide right-angle formation had what appeared to be an elongated submerged lake in it, surrounded by a thin, white beach. Other patterns showed no detail at all—the dark dots seen in the photos were still just dark dots. From the air we had no way of knowing what caused the color patterns, or how deep the water was.

Back on the ground, we focused on our main goal: navigation to the satellite photo patterns from a boat. For the area east of Bimini, where the patterns are located, getting a boat there at all is a challenge. For most people, the idea of an expedition conjures up images of Jacques Cousteau and the *Calypso*. We were a bit smaller scale. We rented a 13-foot Boston Whaler (close kin to a rowboat with an outboard motor), and began our quest. A larger boat would have been useless; we had to cross sand flats in a foot of water, and at times had to climb out and pull the boat. A channel a few inches deeper had been worn away by the propellers of other boats. We followed the "path," and soon reached deeper water. We navigated by compass sightings on the radio tower, by estimating the speed of our boat, and by carefully watching for color changes in the water beneath us.

Within a few minutes, we had found an unquestionable archaeological site. Half-submerged in the water off the tip of the runway on South Bimini was the wreck of an airplane. Smuggling is big business near Bimini, and the area is littered with the wrecks of planes that tried to land at night without lights. But this wasn't Atlantis. We kept on with our search.

The water was about three feet deep, and we began to cross patterns of darker color. We approached one of the "dots" we had seen in the satellite photos. It was a completely circular area, about a hundred yards wide, and black surrounded by white sand. Was it one of the mysterious deep "blue holes" of the Bahamas? To our surprise it wasn't. When we looked under water, all we saw was dense black seagrass, but no change in depth at all. We didn't know what caused the pattern, but there didn't seem to be anything unusual there.

We continued on to one of the most clearly geometric forms on the photos: the rectangle discovered by Valentine. The changes in plant growth on the bottom were striking. Within a few feet, we saw a change between bare sand and thick seagrass. Yet we found no signs of any artifacts or manmade construction. From the water, no one would ever guess at the anomaly revealed from the air. Whatever causes these patterns is buried beneath the sand, perhaps under several feet of sediment; unfortunately, we had no sonar equipment or excavation permits.

The next day, in the same small boat, we traveled more than six miles from shore to find the formation with the "lake" in the middle. This far from shore, Bimini was a faint haze in the distance. From horizon to horizon there was nothing but blue-green water. Once again, the satellite photos were a great help, since they allowed us to use the bottom patterns as a guide to navigation. We didn't have enough time or fuel to look at the entire site, but saw generally what we had seen before: seagrass and sand patterns, with no appearance of sunken buildings.

For the rest of the expedition, we explored on shore and from the air again. Our pilot this time was John Hollis, who had flown his own plane to Bimini with Dr. James Windsor, president of the Edgar Cayce Foundation, and their families. We continued the aerial survey, and went as far south as Ocean Cay, where a sand-mining operation has gouged huge trenches in the sea bottom. In the exploration on shore, we found beachrock forming into large blocks, less than a mile from the road site.

We returned, disappointed at not finding sunken ruins, but pleased that the satellite photos had proved their worth, and ready to make better maps. With satellite-based maps keyed to navigation aids like LORAN, future explorers should have far less difficulty.

Since 1984, plans have been slowly gaining momentum for a general cooperative effort to discover the secrets of Bimini. By 1987, enough interest had been raised to sponsor the Atlantic University Bimini Symposium in Virginia Beach, with which we began the first chapter of this book. The symposium brought together people on all sides of the question, from proponents of some of the wilder stories to orthodox archaeologists. Everyone agreed on two major points: that good mapping was imperative, and that destruction of sites should be avoided. For an archaeologist, the context in which an artifact is found means everything. The new ideal is archaeology in which nothing is touched at all, but first carefully mapped and studied with modern electronic equipment. Remote-sensing techniques such as side-scan sonar and magnetometers are the tools of the new archaeologists. If you want to try your hand at the search, please don't go down with a shovel! Disturbing archaeological sites without a permit is a serious offense. Anyone can search and make discoveries, but leave what you find for future generations. The Atlantic University research department has begun the Bimini Project, which acts as a networking center for explorers, archaeologists, and laypeople with an interest in this area.

Exploration near Bimini has been renewed in earnest, following the Cayce recommendation for a survey that inspired "the geologist" in the 1950s and 1960s. The technology now exists to perform a survey along the edge of the Gulf Stream with side-scan sonar, which could show any buildings projecting above the sea bottom. Even explorers who are not directly part of the Atlantis quest may find sites. As this book is being written, Stephan Schwartz of the Mobius Society in California is conducting an expedition south of Bimini, using both psychics and the high-technology approach. The main purpose of his project is to find shipwrecks, and he has already successfully located several wrecks. With luck, he may find Atlantis as well. Whatever he finds, his approach is the wave of the future. Armed with psychics on the one hand, and high technology on the other, explorers may eventually solve the mystery of Bimini.

Part IV

MIRRORS OF OUR FUTURE

7

ATLANTIS IN OUR FUTURE: EARTHQUAKES?

"ODDS AGAINST US: EARTHQUAKES THREATEN EAST"

A psychic's doomsday warning? No. The above headline is from an editorial by George Hebert, which appeared in the Norfolk, Virginia, *Ledger Star* on February 13, 1987. Hebert's article quoted the results of a recently released American Association of Engineering Societies (AAES) study. It placed the probability of a major quake occurring in the eastern United States (where 80 percent of the people live) at 100 percent by 2010! The major danger areas mentioned coincided with some unusual comments Edgar Cayce gave in readings in 1932 and 1941. This prompted an A.R.E. member to call the newspaper. Within a week, the report, entitled *Vulnerability of Energy Distribution Systems to an Earthquake in the Eastern United States—An Overview*, arrived.

This twenty-six-page report was researched and compiled by the AAES in conjunction with the Coordinating Committee on Energy. Fifty-one references were listed in its bibliography. Some rather disconcerting facts were highlighted in the Executive Summary:

> It is obvious from this paper that research and the study of earthquake damage are still needed to better determine the impact of future earthquakes on energy distribution systems, especially for earthquakes in the

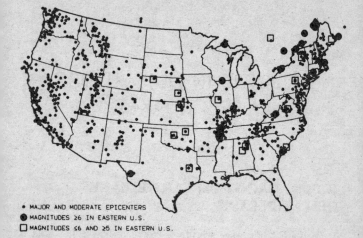

• MAJOR AND MODERATE EPICENTERS
● MAGNITUDES ≥6 IN EASTERN U.S.
□ MAGNITUDES ≤6 AND ≥5 IN EASTERN U.S.

Figure 7-1. Map of major and moderate earthquakes in the United States.

magnitude of 6.0 to 8.0 range. It is also obvious that there is a real threat to the eastern U.S. from the occurrence of some future destructive earthquake. Based on what is known today, the greatest threat lies in the Mississippi Valley, with the next level of concern in the Charleston, S.C. area.

In a worst-case scenario, a repeat of an 1811–1812 earthquake would not only be devastating to the area, but it could have a major impact on the country as well. Although this is believed to be an unlikely event in the next 25 years, as we move into the 21st century the risk becomes much greater.

In conclusion, the earthquake threat to the eastern U.S. is real. Destructive earthquakes have occurred in the past and will occur in the future. The only real uncertainty is where and when. When such an earthquake occurs, it is important that the eastern U.S. be prepared in order to mitigate the effects. This can only be done through effective research, construction, planning and public awareness.

Included with the report were three maps. Figure 7-1 shows major and moderate epicenters (the area on the surface of the earth directly above the origin of an earthquake) in the United States. This map shows danger areas in South Carolina, Georgia, and near New York City. After the Mississippi Valley area, the vicinity of Charleston, S.C., is of great concern.

Compare this information with these quotes from Cayce readings:

Portions of the now east coast of New York, or New York City itself, will in the main disappear. This will be another generation, though, here; while the southern portions of Carolina, Georgia, these will disappear. This will be much sooner. (no. 1152–11, August 13, 1941)

[Q-14.] Will there be any physical changes in the earth's surface in North America? If so, what sections will be affected and how? [A-14.] All over the country we will find many physical changes of a minor or greater degree. The greater change, as we will find in America, will be the North Atlantic Seaboard. Watch New York! Connecticut, and the like. (no. 311–8, April 9, 1932)

As to conditions in the geography of the world, of the country, changes here are gradually coming about. Many portions of the east coast will be disturbed, as well as many portions of the west coast, as well as the central portion of the United States. In the next few years, lands will appear in the Atlantic as well as in the Pacific. And what is the coast line now of many a land will be the bed of the ocean. Even many of the battlefields of the present [1941] will be ocean, will be the seas, the bays, the lands over which the new order will carry on their trade one with another.

The waters of the lakes [Great Lakes] will empty into the gulf [Gulf of Mexico] rather than the waterway over which such discussions have been recently made [St. Lawrence Seaway]. It would be well if the waterway were prepared, but not for that purpose for which it is at present being considered. (no. 1511–11, August 13, 1941)

The AAES report contains two more paragraphs of interest. One compares damage from earthquakes in the eastern and western United States; the other assesses the likelihood of a destructive earthquake occurring in the next twenty-five years.

Our experience in recent times with destructive earthquakes has been on the West Coast. One or more earthquakes of Richter magnitude 6.0 or greater occur somewhere west of the Rocky Mountains each year. The most recent destructive earthquake was the Coalinga earthquake of May 2, 1983, that had a Richter magnitude of 6.5. The most recent significant destructive earthquake was the 1971 San Fernando earthquake, having a Richter magnitude of 6.4. However, neither of these earthquakes impacted as large an area as would be impacted if such an earthquake were to occur in the eastern United States. Figure 7-2 shows the equivalent damage areas of the 1906 San Francisco and 1971 San Fernando earthquakes and the 1811–1812 New Madrid and 1886 Charleston earthquakes. Because of different crustal and geologic conditions that exist in the East, the area impacted is about ten times that in the West. In a rudimentary sense, one can assess that for the same size earthquake the damage would also be about ten times as great in the East, and because the population in the East is larger than in the West, the numbers of people impacted could be much greater depending upon the epicentural location. The large population in the East not only supports the assessment that the damage could be ten times as great, but could even support a value greater than ten.

The likelihood of a destructive earthquake (a magnitude of approximately 6.0 to 6.5) occurring between now and the year 2010 in the New Madrid seismic zone can be estimated to be around 60 percent. The probability of

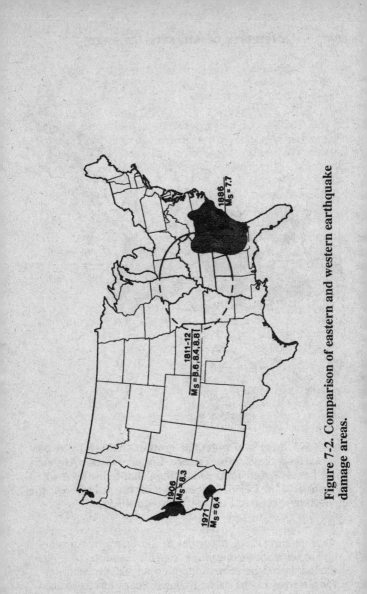

Figure 7-2. Comparison of eastern and western earthquake damage areas.

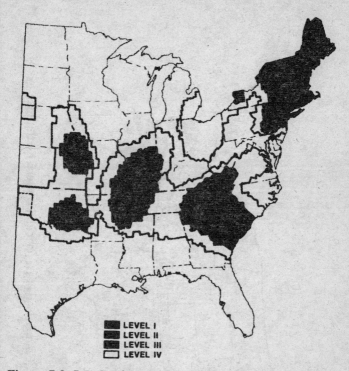

Figure 7-3. Levels of potential ground shaking from possible earthquakes in the eastern United States. (Author's Note: Levels I and II are indistinguishable in the map as published. The Level I area lies in the middle of the darkest area centered on the Mississippi River.)

such an earthquake occurring in the Southern Appalachian seismic zone can be roughly estimated to be around 1 or 3 percent. Adding up all like probabilities for all areas of the eastern United States results in the probability of a destructive earthquake occurring somewhere in the eastern United States in the next 25 years being nearly 100%—an almost sure thing. The only real uncertainty is where it will occur.

Cayce's predictions of earth changes in California and other well-known earthquake zones have received much attention, yet prediction of an earthquake in California at some time in the indeterminate future is not very impressive proof of a psychic's abilities. Yet these predictions of earthquakes in the eastern United States referred to areas that were *not* well known to be danger areas. For many of his earth change predictions, the context was such that Cayce's listeners thought that the changes were imminent in the 1930s; yet they did not come to pass. In other readings, Cayce indicated that the years 1958 to 1998 would see the beginning of the majority of the changes.

What conclusions can we draw from this comparison between the Cayce readings and the latest warnings of geologists? Cayce himself said the future was not fixed, yet clearly the assessment science has put on these prophecies is that the odds are with him 100 percent.

In interpreting a dream of Cayce's in which there were great earth changes, the readings said,

This then is the interpretation. As has been given, ''Fear not.'' Keep the faith; for those that be with thee are greater than those that would hinder. Though the very heavens fall, though the earth shall be changed, though the heavens shall pass, the promises in Him are sure and will stand—as in that day—as the proof of the activity in the lives and hearts of those of thy fellow man . . .

That is the interpretation. That the periods from the material angle as visioned are to come to pass matters not to the soul, but do thy duty *today! Tomorrow* will care for itself.

These changes in the earth will come to pass, for the time and times and half times are at an end, and there begin those periods for the readjustments. For how hath he given? ''The righteous shall inherit the earth.''

Hast thou, my brethren, a heritage in the earth? (no.294–185, June 30, 1936)

AFTERWORD

WAS ATLANTIS A reality?

In this book, we have taken an open-minded look at the Atlantean readings, including their relation to historical sources on Atlantis, occultism, and modern science. Despite his convoluted language and occasional ambiguity, at least some of the time Edgar Cayce seems to have tapped into an accurate vision of past events. Although some readings are vague and rambling, others are concise and straightforward. At times they incorporated popular concepts, yet often with a twist that showed Cayce was trying to guide his listeners to a different point of view. Sometimes he contradicted their preconceptions, as with his persistent explanations that the Egyptian temple of records was not in the Great Pyramid, but in a buried pyramid, yet to be discovered. The dates he gave for past events were far from those accepted in his time, yet in many cases they are now considered quite reasonable.

The scientific evidence is now strong that our clearly identifiable ancestors appeared millions, not thousands of years ago. Early people were widely distributed throughout the world, yet anatomically modern people seem to have appeared after 200,000 years ago, and spread through the world by roughly 50,000 years ago, near the time Cayce gave for the first destruction of Atlantis. Cayce's dates for other destructions of Atlantis closely match those calculated by geologists for magnetic pole reversals, climatic change, earthquakes, volcanic activity, and extinctions. Around 12,000 years ago, after the final destruction, there was a population explosion in the Americas. The *roots* of the great American civilizations (not the final expressions of the classical Maya and Incas) can now be traced back to this time period.

It would have been simple for the authors to have compiled a mildly controversial book, to have listed only Edgar Cayce's ''hits,'' the statements he made years ago that have proved to be accurate. Yet there are still troubling aspects of the readings that simply don't fit with what we know of ancient peoples today. Chief among these is the existence of Atlantis itself. With no confirmed findings of Atlantean ruins, it is hard to convince skeptics that Atlantis was the source of all civilization. There are persistent anomalies—underwater patterns near Bimini, freshwater fossils in the mid-Atlantic—but the temple "under the slime of ages of seawater" in the Cayce readings remains elusive. Likewise the story of Egypt, despite discoveries of possible cavities near the Sphinx, has received a blow from the carbon dating. But the opening of the temple of records could answer many questions. Some of the descriptions of lives in ancient Atlantis also strain the imagination, with their talk of high technology and biological monstrosities. But technology since Cayce's time has shown that these can be real possibilities, however unlikely in the ancient past.

So what are we to make of this tale? Should we accept it all on faith, or dismiss it as lucky guesses? How much credibility can we assign to the Cayce readings?

The answer to this question is quite complex, because there is really no single answer. On different occasions, Cayce seemed to have obtained information of varying quality from different sources. What is true of Cayce in particular is probably true of psychics in general. The variety of sources could have included

- Unconscious memory—material Cayce had read or been told. Many of his biblical quotations certainly came from this source.
- Clairvoyant observations of people and events.
- Telepathic communication between Cayce's mind and those of other individuals. The quality of this information would, of course, depend on the knowledge of the individuals, whether living or dead.
- The Akashic Records, which Cayce said required proper attunement to read. Another way of looking at this is to suppose that Cayce's unconscious mind was able to move in time to see past events as well as future probabilities.

Other influences would have included Cayce's own physical, mental, and emotional states, as well as those of the person who was obtaining the reading, and others involved. Thus the transmission of psychic information was affected much as electrical interference may affect radio and television transmissions.

Just as there are good baseball players, there are good psychics. Edgar Cayce was one of the most accurate psychics of all time, and certainly the best documented. But, just as a baseball player may have a bad night, the best psychic does not always hit 100 percent.

What can we do with this material? The answer from the Cayce readings is not simply to take it on faith, nor to reject it, but to conduct personal or scientific research to determine its validity. In a reading given in 1935 for the then-fledgling Association for Research and Enlightenment, Cayce said, "It's often stated that the work is a research and enlightenment program; but how much research have you done? Isn't it presented rather as enlightenment without much research? Then don't get the cart before the horse! It doesn't work so well! Even with streamlines!" (no. 254–81, January 12, 1935).

This book has been a first step in research, but it is by no means the last word. Whether or not the particulars of the readings are all true, the overall picture being uncovered by archaeology is clear. World history has not been a steady upward climb from the "savage cave man." Many civilizations have risen and fallen over the ages; we are not unique. The Cayce readings add the perspective that we may have risen much higher, and fallen much further, than archaeologists would have believed possible. Could it happen again? And can it be avoided?

Like his descriptions of the past, Cayce's predictions of future probabilities are being confirmed by geologists. Many people are fearfully anticipating destruction by giant earthquakes. Yet Cayce said the future was not fixed, and that even earth changes could be averted. Even in his own day, predictions failed to come to pass, he said, because of changes in the attitudes of people. The story is similar to that of Jonah in the Bible:

God directed Jonah to go to Nineveh and prophesy its destruction because of the wickedness of its inhabitants. Jonah tried to avoid God's call, but, after an experience with a rather large fish, when God called him a second time he did go and proclaimed in the streets of Nineveh its coming doom. Jonah was very persuasive, and the people—from the king on down—became aware of their sins, for they all repented and cried to God for mercy.

"When God saw what they did, how they turned from their evil way, God repented of the evil which he had said he would do to them; and he did not do it" (Jonah 3:10).

Everyone in Nineveh rejoiced except Jonah, who was displeased because his prophecy did not come true!

Are we to be like Jonah, or can we take the message from the Cayce readings that we do not have to go the way of Atlantis?

Even if you believe that at worst Cayce's Atlantean story is a figment of his imagination, and at best it is only an allegory, does it not still have value for us? Who can deny that we are still searching for our relationship to our Maker and our fellow human beings? Is there not a clue in the Atlantean story? The future is not fixed. We have the power to change our destiny, as individuals and as a nation.

Perhaps we are in the position of the comic-strip character Pogo, who said, "We have met the enemy, and he is us." Shall we, like the children of Belial, choose to seek self-gratification, without regard for others? Or shall we, like the children of the Law of One, seek to find the will of God?

Someone once asked Edgar Cayce how to find happiness and peace of mind. He replied, "Aid to others brings release, brings peace, brings harmony. For remember, as His promises were then, they are today: 'My peace I give you, My peace I leave with you, not as the world knoweth peace,' not of ease, but rather that as of the conviction within self that 'Others may do as they may, but as for me, I will serve the living God.' That is the only means, the only outlet, that releases binding forces. For the truth shall make you free and you shall be free indeed!" (no. 2786–1, July 24, 1942).

ATLANTIS UPDATE:
THE SEARCH CONTINUES

SINCE *MYSTERIES OF ATLANTIS REVISITED* was originally published in 1988, scientists have continued to find new evidence that is consistent with the Cayce story of the ancient past. In Egypt, alignments of the pyramids with the stars have shed new light on the Cayce date for Egyptian civilization of about 10,400 B.C. A new chamber has been found in the Great Pyramid that awaits exploration. Another archaeology/geology team in Egypt has uncovered evidence that the Sphinx is far older than traditionally accepted dates—possibly as old as the Cayce readings claim.

New sites in Bimini range from further underwater "roads" to giant mounds in the shape of a shark and other animals. There is even the possibility that the mounds may be aligned with the stars, like the pyramids in Egypt.

There has been an upheaval in anthropology regarding the origins of ancient humanity, making the Cayce story more plausible. The worldwide distribution of human ancestors continues to be pushed further into the past.

Finally, Cayce's prophecies of earth changes may be supported by an apparent increase in the number of major earthquakes, including recent ones in and near Japan.

DISCOVERIES IN EGYPT

New Book Raises Questions About Purpose of Pyramids

In their recent book, *The Orion Mystery* (Crown Publishers, New York, 1994), Robert Bauval and Adrian Gilbert build a case for a new theory of why the pyramids were built. They tie ancient Egyptian religious practices and beliefs to their knowledge of astronomy, claiming that the early Egyptians were familiar with the precession of the stars. Precession is an apparent movement of the stars caused by a wobble of the earth that takes 26,000 years to complete a full cycle. Using computer programs to picture the heavens as they would have appeared from Giza in Egypt, they calculated that the stars in Orion's Belt (in the constellation of Orion) would have been at their lowest point on the horizon in 10,400 B.C. and will be at their highest point in the heavens in A.D. 2550. In another 13,000 years from A.D. 2550 they will have returned to the lowest point, completing the cycle.

The authors claim that the positions of the pyramids on the Giza plateau mirror the positions of the stars in Orion's Belt and call attention to the 10,400 B.C. period as the "first time of Orion." Bauval and Gilbert's mention of the 10,400 B.C. date is interesting as it coincides exactly with Cayce's date of the design and construction of the Great Pyramid and his contention that much of the knowledge of the early Egyptians came from refugees from the sinking of the last remains of the highly technical civilization of Atlantis during that same time period (no. 5748–6, July 1, 1932). Bauval and Gilbert do not say that the Great Pyramid was actually built at this early date, but they identify the date as a significant time in Egyptian history.

New View on the Age of the Sphinx

John Anthony West, writer, guide and amateur archeologist, had long been a proponent of the theory that the Sphinx is much older than commonly thought. The Cayce readings say that the Sphinx was built before the pyramids, prior to 10,500 B.C. (no. 5748–5, June 30, 1932). Egyptologists think it was constructed around 2500 B.C. by Pharaoh Chephren, and that its head bears his likeness. West's reasons for believing they are wrong are:

1. *Different weathering of the Sphinx and Old Kingdom tombs*. The Sphinx is weathered dramatically, with channels over two feet deep worn into its sides. Tombs belonging to Chephren's period and cut into

the same layer of bedrock directly north and south of the Sphinx do not show such weathering. If the tombs and the Sphinx were built at the same time the weathering should be similar.

2. *Evidence of different stages of construction of the Sphinx and Valley Temples.* The temples in front of the Sphinx seem to have been built in two stages, with granite blocks covering an inner core of weathered limestone. If the granite blocks are attributed to Chephren (which no one questions) then the inner core of huge weathered limestone blocks must be older.

3. *Evidence of repair to the Sphinx in Old Kingdom times.* The earliest repairs carried out on the Sphinx show typical Old Kingdom masonry. All significant weathering to the Sphinx took place before these repairs. If the Sphinx was first repaired in Old Kingdom times (when the pyramids were supposed to have been built) it means it must be older.

4. *Different styles.* The architectural style of the Sphinx and of the temples in front of it is different from that of other Old Kingdom structures. In art history there is generally a prevailing architecture/artistic style dominant in any given time. Changes in style allow art historians to assign dates to buildings, paintings and sculptures. The difference in style between Old Kingdom architecture and the Sphinx is enough to convince art historians that different epochs are involved.

West finally found support for his beliefs from two credible, though unrelated sources. One source, Frank Domingo, a New York police detective and a specialist in forensic portraiture, reconstructed the face of the Sphinx. Using standard forensic procedures, he compared it to a portrait of the Pharaoh Chephren. He concluded there were few similarities and that the head of the Sphinx was *not* a representation of Chephren.

Though this in itself does not support an earlier age for the Sphinx, it does raise provocative questions.

West's second source, Robert Schoch, a Yale-trained geologist now at Boston University, examined the weathering of the Sphinx carefully. With the aid of seismologist Thomas Dobecki, from the Colorado School of Mines, he looked at the erosion pattern of the base of the Sphinx above and below the level of the surrounding sand. Schoch described the erosion pattern of the base as a deep, rolling, undulating weathered surface, indicative of *water erosion.* It was very different from the wind and sand erosion pattern of other structures on the Giza Plateau. When the erosion pattern at the base of the Sphinx was compared to tombs and related structures, cut from the identical bedrock as the Sphinx and *attributed to the same time period,* the erosion patterns were different. The tombs and other structures exhibited a pattern of erosion from wind and sand, *not water.* There is evidence that the general area was moist from about 10,000 B.C. to about 5,000 B.C. It has gotten dryer ever since then. Because the area has been very dry for thousands of years, erosion by water must have occurred in earlier times. Thus the Sphinx itself must be thousands of years older than is commonly believed.

Schoch believes the Sphinx must date from 5000 to 7000 B.C. West holds out for an even earlier date. Certainly Cayce's date of prior to 10,500 B.C. has become more credible!

Schoch adds another argument to support his case. On the Sakkara Plateau, within sight of the Giza Plateau, are beautifully preserved mud brick mastabas or tombs, dated to 2700 to 2800 B.C. Since these two plateaus are only a few miles apart, the same weather conditions must have prevailed on Sakkara as on Giza over the past centuries. If there had been enough precipitation since 2500 B.C. to weather and erode the base of the Sphinx as it is eroded, how did the mud brick mastabas survive? Schoch concludes the Sphinx must have been built long before the mud brick mastabas.

Schoch presented his findings to the Geological Society of America Convention in San Diego in October of 1991, and published them in an article in *Omni* magazine in August 1992. Immediately a controversy arose between geologists and Egyptologists. The Egyptologists claim they have found no evidence of a culture dating that far back in Egypt's past capable of creating such a structure as the Sphinx. Geologists say the facts speak for themselves and that because no culture has been found does not prove that one did not exist. If the geologists are right, then much of what Egyptologists think they know would have to be wrong. Schoch and West achieved prime-time notoriety with the television documentary, *Mystery of the Sphinx* in the fall of 1993.

The heated debate has continued in the archaeology journals. The September/October 1994 issue of *Archaeology* magazine devoted 16 pages to a rebuttal of West's and Schoch's ideas by Mark Lehner and Zahi Hawass, prominent experts in Egyptology. Lehner and Hawass raise questions about the geology of the Sphinx and surrounding area that can only be answered by further research.

An interesting sidebar to the controversy is that Dobecki claims his seismic studies detected cavities or chambers beneath the Sphinx and *between its paws*. These anomalies have yet to be investigated. Could they be related to Cayce's "Hall of Records" (no. 5748–6, July 31, 1932), discussed in detail previously in our chapter on Egypt?

Evidence for Hidden Chamber Discovered in Great Pyramid

The most recent discovery in Egypt was reported in February 1994, in an English newspaper, *The Independent*. A group of German scientists, investigating the circulation of the air in the Great Pyramid, sent a robot camera up a small inclined shaft. Much to their amazement they found the 45 degree shaft blocked, after about 65 meters, by a door, complete with two copper handles. The door looked to be made of alabaster or yellow limestone, and of a portcullis design, that could be opened by sliding it upwards into a cavity.

Around a very small opening between the door and the stone wall of the passageway the camera revealed a small scattering of fine black dust. This dust could not have come from the yellow stone of the passageway or the door itself. It was, however, typical of decaying organic material, especially wood or textiles. Tutankhamen's tomb and others have yielded

The Great Pyramid

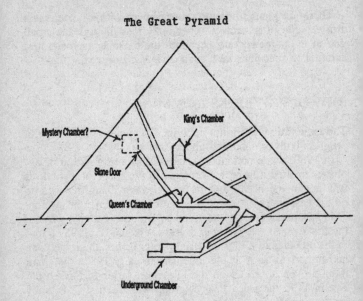

huge numbers of wooden objects and textiles, including coffins and cloth used to wrap mummified corpses. The fact that the black dust had been blown out of the small crack implied the existence of air currents beyond the door. This in turn suggests the existence of a large chamber behind the door.

To further substantiate the idea of a large chamber is the fact that the door is exactly 21.5 meters higher than the largest known chamber in the pyramid, the King's Chamber. The King's Chamber in turn is exactly 21.5 meters higher than the Queen's Chamber, the second largest known chamber in the pyramid. This has raised speculation that the mystery chamber may contain treasures rivaling that of Tutankhamen's tomb, or even the body of a Pharaoh. This is pure speculation though, for both the King's and Queen's Chambers were empty when they were discovered. Even the sarcophagus in the King's Chambers was devoid of a body. It is not known whether these chambers were once packed with artifacts that were subsequently looted, or if they have always been empty.

There are plans to fit the robot camera with an extendable arm capable of inserting a fiber optic lens through the small gap in the stonework to peer into the chamber beyond. It is exciting to speculate what such a view may reveal.

NEW DISCOVERIES IN BIMINI

The exploration of Bimini continues to gain momentum, with progress both on land and underwater.

In 1989, while conducting an aerial survey, a group of explorers spotted a large sand mound in the shape of a shark. It was not in the ocean, but in the saltwater mangrove swamp on the east side of Bimini, rising a few feet above the swamp. This group, the Gaea Project, led by Dr. Joan Hanley, was not the first ever to see the mound. It was evident on a 1957 photo in the archives of a Florida aerial photographer, though no one had remarked on it at the time. In the early 1980s the shark mound even appeared on the television series *In Search Of.* But in 1990 the Gaea Project group was the first to actually set foot on it.

Deep in a featureless swamp of dense mangrove trees, the mound is difficult to find and explore. From a boat, the numerous channels crisscrossing the swamp all look alike. The group [including one of the authors of this book, Douglas Richards] carried aerial photos taken the previous year to aid in navigation, using small mangrove islands as landmarks.

The shark mound, about 500 feet long by 100 feet wide, and 10 feet high, resembles the "effigy" mounds of North America. One of the most famous effigy mounds is the serpent mound in Ohio, which is almost exactly the same size as the shark mound in length and height. These effigy mounds date back to perhaps 1000 B.C. or earlier. As yet, we have no way of dating the shark mound.

The shark mound is not alone in the mangrove swamps. Nearby is a mound roughly rectangular in shape, about 200 by 400 feet. Adjacent to it is another mound which looks somewhat like a cat, complete with "eyes"—round areas of sand not covered by vegetation. The Gaea project received a permit from the Bahamas government to explore the mounds to determine their age and whether or not they are man-made. Dr. Claude Swanson, a physicist in the group, brought in ground-penetrating radar to probe beneath the mound. Unfortunately, this radar does not penetrate salt water, and the water table is only a couple feet beneath the surface, so little was learned about the underlying structure. Cores have been drilled down several feet, but so far have found only sand and no datable human artifacts. The Gaea Project continues this work, and hopes to have answers about the origin and age of the mounds in the near future.

Underwater exploration continues as well. When the original edition of this book was written in 1988, it was clear that the Cayce readings recommended a geological survey of the Gulf Stream near Bimini, far offshore from where most of the exploration had been done (no. 364–3, February 16, 1932). Between Bimini and Florida, approximately a mile from Bimini, is an abrupt dropoff from about 60 feet to several hundred feet. This is too deep for aerial photography to reveal anything, and the depth and swift currents also make scuba diving difficult. But it is geologically certain that in 10,000 B.C. this area was all above water—the coastline of a large island.

In 1994, as part of a television production for the Discovery Channel [*Secrets of The Deep: The Hunt For Atlantis*], the Gaea Project was able to use side-scan sonar to probe the depths. In even the small area that was covered, numerous anomalous features appeared—projections above the bottom that could be coral, shipwrecks or even sunken buildings. Only further exploration by divers and underwater cameras will reveal what lies below.

Finally, in early 1995, a Gaea Project group explored some large stone formations uncovered by Hurricane Andrew, several miles south of Bimini. In appearance they are similar to the controversial "road" site off North Bimini. Whether or not they are of human origin remains to be determined. The Gaea Project plans further exploration.

Astronomical Alignments of The Mounds?

As discussed earlier, Robert Bauval has shown that not only are the pyramids aligned to the stars, but that Cayce's date of about 10,400 B.C. is encoded astronomically in the pyramids. Could the mounds in Bimini be aligned to the stars above? One of the Cayce Bimini readings is intriguing, given for the woman aviator who found the healing well on North Bimini. She asked how the well could be promoted and reconstructed. Part of the answer included the following statement:

"This should *not* be left alone; It should be considered from many angles." (no. 587–4, July 1, 1935)

The mounds are in the mangrove swamps of North Bimini, in the general area where Cayce located the well. The tail of the shark mound and the entire rectangular mound are highly geometrical. The tail of the shark mound has sides making a right angle, oriented north-south, east-west. The rectangular mound isn't actually a perfect rectangle; the sides aren't quite parallel, and one of them is oriented north-south. Could the angles of these mounds have further astronomical significance, like those of some of the mounds of the North American Indians (the "Mound Builders")?

One obstacle to answering the question was the lack of a good land survey. However, an aerial photo commissioned by surveyor Raymond Leigh, combined with a topographic map published in the Bahamas, made it possible to orient the mounds fairly accurately. It was possible to measure the angles with respect to true north made by the geometrical patterns of the mounds. Then, the same computer program employed by Bauval, the SkyGlobe program, could be used to look for astronomical alignments.

Several alignments appeared, in addition to the obvious north-south, east-west alignments. Because we do not know the date of the mounds' construction, however, it is difficult to know how valid these alignments may be. It appears that the major angles of the site would have pointed to the brightest stars in the sky (Sirius, Rigel, Vega, Capella and others) at about A.D. 1000. This is much too recent to be an Atlantean site, but very consistent with the dates for the mounds of North America.

Reading 587–4 said "It could be established as a center for . . . archaeological research." Perhaps Cayce was referring to multiple archaeological sites, from Atlantis to the inhabitants of the Bahamas when Columbus arrived. We will need accurate dates for the sites and better surveys before we can say for sure.

HUMAN ORIGINS

Some of the Cayce material appearing most unlikely in Cayce's time was his description of human origins and the antiquity of humanity. His dates were far more ancient than any accepted by science. In Cayce's time the human race was thought to be at most a few thousand years old. But the readings mention ancestors as far back as 10 million years ago, and high civilization 200,000 years ago (no. 364-4, February 16, 1932).

In the first edition of this book, we showed how some of Cayce's statements seem far more reasonable in the light of modern science. New discoveries are constantly pushing the dates for human ancestors and the origin of civilization back further into the past. According to an Associated Press story in the *Virginian-Pilot* (September 22, 1994), "Fossils from Africa May Be Missing Link," a potential human ancestor has been dated at 4.4 million years old.

There also continues to be evidence for ancient technology. An article in *Science News* (May 6, 1995), "Stone Age Fabric Leaves Swatch Marks," shows how even in the Stone Age there may have been sophisticated technology that simply did not preserve well. Pottery fragments from 27,000 years ago in Europe have been found with impressions of woven fabric. The article quotes researchers as saying, "We never anticipated that there was a fiber technology so long ago." This find pushes the earliest date for textiles back 10,000 years further into the past. While this discovery is still a long way from the sort of high technology described in the Cayce readings, it is also a long way from the concept of primitive, brutish cavemen popular in Cayce's time.

How did modern humans first appear? Cayce spoke of the races appearing simultaneously in different parts of the world (no. 364-13, November 17, 1932). When we wrote the first edition of this book in 1988, some anthropologists considered this a possibility, but it was decidedly a minority viewpoint. The majority felt that humanity originated in Africa, perhaps 200,000 years ago, and then migrated throughout the world.

There have been huge changes in mainstream opinion in a short eight years. *Time* magazine described it as "an anthropological ruckus." The *Time* cover story for March 14, 1994 was titled, "How Man Began." *Time* said, "Fossil bones from the dawn of humanity are rewriting the story of human evolution." New fossils, not apelike human ancestors, but the genus *Homo*—our own genus—are being found throughout the world as much as 1.8 million years ago! Now, many anthropologists feel that these early humans, *Homo erectus*, evolved to modern humans, *Homo sapiens*, in a number of places at once, rather than migrating from Africa. Virtually every week new discoveries are made, further complicating the picture of human origins. Cayce's vision is surprisingly supported much of the time.

EARTHQUAKES: UPDATE

Has earthquake activity increased since this book was originally published in 1988? Information on numbers of earthquakes is provided by the United States Geographical Service/National Earthquake Information Center. Their database separates quakes by magnitude, with higher magnitudes denoting more damaging earthquakes. We compared the numbers for 1984–1988 with the numbers for 1989–1993. In most magnitude categories, there seems to be an increase.

For light earthquakes (less than magnitude 6) it is difficult to tell whether this is a real increase or not, because the number of seismograph stations has increased. More seismograph stations record more nearby small earthquakes, so although the numbers have increased, it may be due to better coverage.

For major and strong earthquakes, however, the answer seems to be yes. Earthquakes of this size would be recognized from recording stations worldwide. As the following table shows, there has been a 49% increase in the number of major earthquakes (magnitude 7.0 to 7.9) and a 10% increase in the number of strong earthquakes (magnitude 6.0 to 6.9).

Magnitude	Total 1984–1988	Total 1989–1993	% Increase
7.0 to 7.9	45	67	49%
6.0 to 6.9	495	544	10%

Two large 1995 quakes—one in Kobe, Japan and the other just off Japan on Sakhalin Island in Russia—make one wonder about this quote from the readings:

"The greater portion of Japan must go into the sea . . . And these will begin in those periods in '58 to '98." (no. 3976–15, January 19, 1934)

At this point, only time will prove or disprove the accuracy of the Cayce prophecies, and 1998 is drawing near.

SUMMARY

The hard evidence for Atlantis—underwater temples and buildings—continues to be elusive. But the trend in new discoveries, from Egypt to Bimini, tends to make the Cayce readings more plausible. The deeper science probes, the more anomalies appear to complicate our picture of the ancient past.

SELECTED BIBLIOGRAPHY

Aldred, C. *The Egyptians*. London: Thames and Hudson, 1984.

Ani, Hunefer, Anhai. *The Book of the Dead* (with commentary by Evelyn Rossiter). London: British Museum, 1978.

Anonymous (Geologist). *Earth Changes*. Virginia Beach, Virginia: A.R.E. Press, 1959. Reprinted in H. L. Cayce, *Earth Changes Update*. Virginia Beach, Virginia: A.R.E. Press, 1982.

Berlitz, C. *The Mysteries of Atlantis*. New York: Grosset & Dunlap, 1969.

———. *Atlantis, the Eighth Continent*. New York: G. P. Putnam's Sons, 1984.

Blavatsky, H. P. *The Secret Doctrine*. London: Theosophical Publishing House, 1971.

Bramwell, J. *Lost Atlantis*. London: Cobden-Sanderson, 1937.

Brested, J. H. *A History of the Ancient Egyptians*. New York: Charles Scribner's Sons, 1919.

Budge, E. A. W. *The Book of the Kings of Egypt*. Vol. 1, Dynasties I–XIX. London: Kegan Paul, Trench, Trubner & Co., Ltd., 1908.

Cayce, E. E. *Edgar Cayce on Atlantis*. New York: Paperback Library (Warner Books), 1968.

———. *Humor from the Edgar Cayce Readings*. Virginia Beach, Virginia: A.R.E. Press, 1980.

Cayce, E. E., and H. L. Cayce. *The Outer Limits of Edgar Cayce's Power*. New York: Harper & Row, 1971.

Cayce, H. L. *Earth Changes Update*. Virginia Beach, Virginia: A.R.E. Press, 1980.

———. *Venture Inward*. New York: Harper & Row, 1964.

Ceram, C. W. *Gods, Graves and Scholars*. (Translated from the German by E. B. Garfield.) New York: Alfred A. Knopf, 1954.

Churchward, J. *The Lost Continent of Mu*. New York: Ives & Washburn, 1931.

Coon, C. S. *The Origin of Races*. New York: Alfred A. Knopf, 1962.

de Camp, L. Sprague. *Lost Continents*. New York: Gnome Press, 1954.

Donnelly, I. *Atlantis, the Antediluvian World*. (Revised by Egerton Sykes.) New York: Harper & Brothers, 1949.

Dunbar, C. O. *Historical Geology*. New York: Wiley, 1949.

Fix, W. *The Bone Peddlers*. New York: Macmillan, 1984.

Goodman, J. *American Genesis*. New York: Summit Books, 1981.
————. *Psychic Archeology*. New York: G. P. Putnam's Sons, 1977.
Hassam, S. *Excavations at Giza*. Cairo, Egypt: Cairo Government Press, 1930–1939.
Hay, C. L., R. L. Linton, S. K. Lathrop, H. L. Shapiro, and G. C. Vaillant, eds. *The Mayas and Their Neighbors*. New York: Dover, 1977 (originally published 1940).
Heyerdahl, T. *Early Man and the Oceans*. New York: Random House, 1978.
Hitching, F. *The Neck of the Giraffe: Darwin, Evolution and the New Biology*. New York: New American Library, 1982.
James, T. G. H. *Excavating in Egypt*. Chicago: University of Chicago Press, 1982.
Jennings, J. D. *Prehistory of North America*. 2d ed. New York: McGraw-Hill, 1974.
Johanson, D., and M. Edey. *Lucy: The Beginnings of Humankind*. New York: Warner Books, 1981.
Johnson, P. *The Civilizations of Ancient Egypt*. New York: Atheneum, 1978.
Kukal, Z. *Atlantis in the Light of Modern Research*. Amsterdam, Netherlands: Elsevier, 1984.
Lehner, M. *The Egyptian Heritage*. Virginia Beach, Virginia: A.R.E. Press, 1974.
Ley, W. *Another Look at Atlantis*. Garden City, New York: Doubleday, 1970.
Lyell, C. *Principles of Geology*. London: John Murray, 1853.
McIntyre, L. *The Incredible Incas and Their Timeless Land*. Washington, D.C.: National Geographical Society, 1975.
Martin, P. S., and R. G. Klein, eds. *Quaternary Extinctions: A Prehistoric Revolution*. Tucson: University of Arizona Press, 1984.
Mavor, J. *Voyage to Atlantis*. New York: G. P. Putnam's Sons, 1969.
Mendelsohn, K. *Riddles of the Pyramids*. New York: Praeger, 1974.
Mercer, S. B. *The Pyramid Texts*. Vols. II and IV. New York: Longman's, Green and Co., 1952.
Oliver, F. (Phylos the Tibetan). *Dweller on Two Planets*. Los Angeles: Poseid Publishing, 1920.
Petrie, W. M. F. *The Religion of Ancient Egypt*. London: Constable & Co., Ltd., 1912.
Reisner, G. A. *Giza Necropolis*. (Revised by William S. Smith.) Cambridge, Massachusetts: Harvard University Press, 1955.
Scott-Elliot, W. *The Story of Atlantis and the Lost Lemuria*. London: Theosophical Publishing House, 1925.
Shangle, R. D., and L. Kelso. *Volcano*. Beaverton, Oregon: Beautiful America Publishing Co., 1980.

Shutler, R., Jr., ed. *Early Man in the New World.* Beverly Hills: Sage Publications, 1983.

Silverberg, R. *The Mound Builders.* New York: Ballantine Books, 1970.

Spence, L. *Atlantis in America.* New York: David McKay, 1928.

Stearn, J. *Edgar Cayce—The Sleeping Prophet.* New York: Doubleday, 1967.

Steiner, R. *Atlantis and Lemuria.* London: Anthroposophical Publishing Co., 1923.

Stemman, R. *Atlantis and the Lost Lands.* Garden City, New York: Doubleday, 1977.

Streuver, S., and F. A. Holton. *Koster: Americans in Search of Their Prehistoric Past.* Garden City, New York: Doubleday/Anchor Press, 1979.

Sugrue, T. *There Is a River.* New York: Henry Holt & Co., 1942.

Sullivan, W. *Continents in Motion.* New York: McGraw-Hill, 1979.

Van Sertima, I. *They Came Before Columbus.* New York: Random House, 1976.

Von Wauthenau, A. *Unexpected Faces in Ancient America.* New York: Crown Publishers, 1982.

Vyse, H. *Operations Carried On at the Pyramids of Gizeh in 1837.* London: J. Fraser, 1840–1842.

Wauchope, R. *Lost Tribes and Sunken Continents.* Chicago: University of Chicago Press, 1962.

Wegener, A. *The Origins of Continents and Oceans.* Translated by John Birams. New York: Dover, 1966 (originally published 1929).

White, J. *Pole Shift.* Garden City, New York: Doubleday, 1980.

Zhirov, N. *Atlantis, Atlantology: Basic Problems.* Moscow, USSR: Progress Publishers, 1970.

Zink, D. *The Stones of Atlantis.* Englewood Cliffs, New Jersey: Prentice-Hall, 1978.

PERIODICALS

Adovasio, J. M., D. Gunn, J. Donahue, and R. Stuckenrath. 1978. Meadowcroft Rockshelter, 1977: an overview. *American Antiquity* 43:632–51.

Allen, J. P., K. L. Gauri, and M. Lehner. 1980. The ARCE Sphinx Project: a preliminary report. *American Research Center in Egypt Newsletter*, no. 112, pp. 3–33.

Anonymous. 1977. Unique volcanic subsea specimens. *Science News* 111:102.

Barbetti, M., and M. McElhinney. 1972. Evidence of a geomagnetic excursion 30,000 yr b.p. *Nature* 239:327–30.

Bower, B. 1986. People in Americas before last ice age? *Science News* 129:405–6.

Clausen, C. J., et al. 1979. Little Salt Spring, Florida: A unique underwater site. *Science* 203:604–14.

Cruxent, J., and I. Rouse. 1969. Early man in the West Indies. *Scientific American* 221 (11, November): 42–52.

Edwards, R. L., and K. O. Emery. 1977. Man on the continental shelf. *Annals of the New York Academy of Sciences* 228:245–56.

Emiliani, C. 1976. The great flood. *Sea Frontiers* (Sept.–Oct.): 259–70.

Emiliani, C., et al. 1975. Paleoclimatological analysis of late Quaternary cores from the Northeastern Gulf of Mexico. *Science* 189:1083–88.

Fairbridge, R. W. 1977. Global climate change during the 13,500-b.p. Gothenburg geomagnetic excursion. *Nature* 265:430–31.

Falk, D. 1983. Cerebral cortices of East African early Hominids. *Science* 221:1072–74.

Feder, K. 1980. Psychic archaeology, the anatomy of irrationalist prehistoric studies. *The Skeptical Inquirer* 4(4):32–43.

———. 1983. America disingenuous: Goodman's "American Genesis"—a new chapter in "cult" archaeology. *The Skeptical Inquirer* 7(4):36–48.

Flohn, H. 1979. On time scales and causes of abrupt paleoclimatic events. *Quaternary Research* 12:135–49.

Gauri, K. L. 1981. Deterioration of the stone of the Great Sphinx. *American Research Center in Egypt Newsletter*, no. 114, pp. 35–47.

Gifford, J. A., and M. M. Ball. 1980. Investigation of submerged beachrock deposits off Bimini, Bahamas. *National Geographic Society Research Reports* 12:21–38.

Gold, T. 1955. Instability of the earth's axis of rotation. *Nature* 175: 526–29.

Greenman, E. F. 1963. The Upper Palaeolithic and the New World. *Current Anthropology* 4:41–91.

Guidon, N., and G. Delabrias. 1986. Carbon-14 dates point to man in the Americas 32,000 years ago. *Nature* 321: 769–71.

Hamblin, D. J. 1986. A unique approach to unraveling the secrets of the Great Pyramids. *Smithsonian* 17 (April): 78–93.

Harrison, W. 1971. Atlantis undiscovered: Bimini, Bahamas. *Nature* 230:287–89.

Haynes, V. 1973. The Calico site: artifacts or geofacts? *Science* 181: 305–9.

Kennett, J. P., and N. D. Watkins. 1970. Geomagnetic polarity change, volcanic maxima, and faunal extinction in the South Pacific. *Nature* 227:930–34.

Kerr, R. 1986. Ancient river system across Africa proposed. *Science* 233:940.

Kolbe, R. W. 1957. Fresh-water diatoms from Atlantic deep-sea sediments. *Science* 126:1053–56.

———. 1958. Turbidity currents and displaced fresh-water diatoms. *Science* 127:1504.

Leakey, L. S. B., R. E. Simpson, and T. Clements. 1968. Archaeological excavations in the Calico Mountains, California: Preliminary report. *Science* 160:1022–23.

Lehner, M. 1983. Some observations on the layout of the Khufu and Khafre pyramids. *Journal of the ARCE* 20: 7–25.

Lewin, R. 1985. The Taung baby reaches sixty. *Science* 227:1188–90.

———. 1987. Africa: Cradle of modern humans. *Science* 237:1292–95.

Lindstrom, T. 1980. SEAS Bimini ('71,'72,'79) and Quintana Roo ('74,'75,'79) expeditions. *The Epigraphic Society, Occasional Publications* 8, Pt. 2:189–98.

———. 1982. Bimini marine archaeological expedition. *Explorers Journal* (March):25–9.

McKusick, M. 1984. Psychic archaeology from Atlantis to Oz. *Archaeology* 37(5):48–52.

McKusick, M., and E. A. Shinn. 1980. Bahamian Atlantis reconsidered. *Nature* 287:11–12.

MacNeish, R. S. 1971. Early man in the Andes. *Scientific American* 224(4):36–46.

——. 1976. Early man in the New World. *American Scientist* 64: 316–27.

Marshack, A. 1975. Exploring the mind of ice age man. *National Geographic* 147 (1, January): 62–89.

Martin, P. S. 1966. Africa and pleistocene overkill. *Nature* 212:339–42.

Milliman, J. D., and K. O. Emery. 1968. Sea levels during the past 35,000 years. *Science* 162:1121–23.

Morner, N. -A., and J. Lanser. 1974. Gothenburg magnetic "flip." *Nature* 251:408–9.

Oakley, K. P., and J. S. Weiner. 1955. Piltdown man. *American Scientist* 43:573–83.

Poulton, J. 1987. All about Eve. *New Scientist* 1560. (14 May 1987): 51–3.

Rebikoff, D. 1979. Underwater archaeology: photogrammetry of artifacts near Bimini. *Explorers Journal* (September): 122–25.

Rigby J. K., and L. H. Burckle. 1958. Turbidity currents and displaced fresh-water diatoms. *Science* 127:1504.

Rogers, R. A. 1985. Glacial geography and native North American languages. *Quaternary Research* 23:130–37.

Shinn, E. A. 1978. Atlantis: Bimini hoax. *Sea Frontiers* 24:130–41.

Solecki, R. S. 1975. Shanidar IV, a Neanderthal flower burial in Northern Iraq. *Science* 190:880–81.

Steen-McIntyre, V., R. Fryxell, and H. E. Malde. 1981. Geological evidence for age of deposits at Hueyatlaco archaeological site, Valsequillo, Mexico. *Quaternary Research* 16:1–17.

Straus, L. G. 1985. Stone age prehistory of northern Spain. *Science* 230:501–7.

Turner, C. G., II. 1982. American Genesis: The American Indian and the origins of modern man by Jeffrey Goodman. *Archaeology* 35(1): 72–4.

——. 1986. Dentochronological separation estimates for Pacific Rim populations. *Science* 232:1140–42.

Valentine, J. M. 1976. Underwater archaeology in the Bahamas. *Explorers Journal* (December): 176–83.

Van Elderen, B. 1979. The Nag Hammadi excavation. *Biblical Archaeologist* 42 (Fall): 225–31.

Warlow, P. 1978. Geomagnetic reversals? *Journal of Physics, A* 11 (7 October 1978):2107–30.

Wendorf, F., et al. 1975. Dates for the middle stone age of East Africa. *Science* 187:740–42.

Whitmore, F. C., Jr., et al. 1967. Elephant teeth on the Atlantic Continental Shelf. *Science* 156:1477–81.

Willey, G. R. 1982. Maya archaeology. *Science* 215:260–67.

INDEX

ABOUT THE AUTHORS

Edgar Evans Cayce is the youngest son of Edgar Cayce. He graduated from Duke University in 1939 with a B.S. in electrical engineering, and is a registered professional engineer in Virginia. He is retired after 43 years of service with the Virginia Power Company. Edgar Evans Cayce is the author of *Edgar Cayce on Atlantis*, and coauthor, with Hugh Lynn Cayce, of *The Outer Limits of Edgar Cayce's Power*. He is a member of the Board of Trustees of the Edgar Cayce Foundation, the Association for Research and Enlightenment, and Atlantic University.

Gail Cayce Schwartzer is the granddaughter of Edgar Cayce and daughter of Edgar Evans Cayce. She graduated from Ohio State University in 1968 with a B.S. in psychology. She worked with the Edgar Cayce Foundation for 15 years, and is the author of *Osteopathy—Comparative Concepts of A. T. Still and Edgar Cayce*.

Douglas G. Richards is Director of Research for Atlantic University in Virginia Beach, Virginia. He has a Ph.D. in biology from the University of North Carolina. In 1976 and 1984 he participated in expeditions to the island of Bimini in the Bahamas in search of the ruins of Atlantis. He is the author of numerous scientific papers, including "Water Penetration Aerial Photography" in the *International Journal of Nautical Archaeology and Underwater Exploration*.

EDGAR CAYCE'S WISDOM FOR THE NEW AGE

More information from the Edgar Cayce readings is available to you on hundreds of topics from astrology and arthritis to universal laws and world affairs, because Cayce established an organization, the Association for Research and Enlightenment (A.R.E.), to preserve his readings and make the information available to everyone.

Today over seventy-five thousand members of the A.R.E. receive a bimonthly magazine, *Venture Inward*, containing articles on dream interpretation, past lives, health and diet tips, psychic archaeology, psi research, book reviews, and interviews with leaders and authors in the metaphysical field. Members also receive extracts of medical and nonmedical readings and may do their own research in all of the over fourteen thousand readings that Edgar Cayce gave during his lifetime.

To receive more information about the association that continues to research and make available information on subjects in the Edgar Cayce readings, please write A.R.E., Dept. M13, P.O: Box 595, Virginia Beach, VA 23451, or call (804) 428-3588. The A.R.E. will be happy to send you a packet of materials describing its current activities.